Praise for *The Genius Zone*

"Imagine sitting down with the coaching legend Gay Hendricks as he works his transformational magic with you! Reading his new book, *The Genius Zone*, is just like that. He's truly a genius at giving us the tools to unleash our own genius."　　　—Arielle Ford, author of
*The Soulmate Secret*

"The inner intelligence of the body is the ultimate and supreme genius. Gay shows how to connect with this inner intelligence and discover the secrets to healing, love, intuition, and insight."　　　—Deepak Chopra

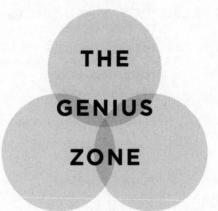

THE

GENIUS

ZONE

## ALSO BY GAY HENDRICKS

*The Big Leap*

*Conscious Loving*

*Five Wishes*

*Conscious Living*

*The Corporate Mystic*

*At the Speed of Life*

*Learning to Love Yourself*

*Conscious Luck*

# THE
# GENIUS
# ZONE

## The Breakthrough Process
## to End Negative Thinking and
## Live in True Creativity

## GAY HENDRICKS

ST. MARTIN'S
**ESSENTIALS**
NEW YORK

First published in the United States by St. Martin's Essentials,
an imprint of St. Martin's Publishing Group.

THE GENIUS ZONE. Copyright © 2021 by The Hendricks Institute. All rights
reserved. Printed in the United States of America. For information, address
St. Martin's Publishing Group, 120 Broadway, New York, NY 10271.

www.stmartins.com

Designed by Jonathan Bennett

Library of Congress Cataloging-in-Publication Data

Names: Hendricks, Gay, author.
Title: The genius zone : the breakthrough process to end negative thinking
    and live in true creativity / Gay Hendricks.
Other titles: Joy of genius
Description: First edition. | New York : St. Martin's Essentials, [2021] |
    Originally published by Waterside Press in 2018 under the title
    The Joy of Genius.
Identifiers: LCCN 2021002070 | ISBN 9781250246547 (hardcover) |
    ISBN 9781250622617 (ebook)
Subjects: LCSH: Success. | Success in business. | Creative thinking.
Classification: LCC BF637.S8 H3924 2021 | DDC 158.1—dc23
LC record available at https://lccn.loc.gov/2021002070

Our books may be purchased in bulk for promotional, educational,
or business use. Please contact your local bookseller or the Macmillan
Corporate and Premium Sales Department at 1-800-221-7945, extension
5442, or by email at MacmillanSpecialMarkets@macmillan.com.

A version of this book was originally published by
Waterside Press in 2018 under the title *The Joy of Genius*

First Edition: 2021

10  9  8  7  6  5  4  3  2  1

*For Katie—mate, muse, and best friend*

# Contents

# Introduction

## LIVING IN YOUR GENIUS ZONE

Welcome to one of the most important conversations a conscious human being ever has: how to live your whole life in a continuous upward spiral of your creative genius.

I've been richly blessed to have had thousands of conversations about genius with students and colleagues around the world. In my book *The Big Leap*, I shared the key findings from my first three decades of exploration into how human beings can optimize the gifts they have been given.

Since *The Big Leap* came out, I've discovered several powerful new tools for evoking your genius. Specifically, I want to give you detailed instructions on how to use the most essential technique, a tool you can use in a split second to stop recycling problems and create a life centered in your genius.

## The Meta-Tool

In the first part of this book, you will learn how to spot what I call the *Genius Moment* and how to use a specific tool called the *Genius Move*. The Genius Moment is an opening, an invitation to bring forth your highest potential. You get hundreds of Genius Moments every day, each one an opportunity to make the Genius Move and step through into the life you really want to live.

The Genius Move is a body-mind tool you can apply in the blink of an eye. Each time you use it you create more open space through which your genius can be accessed and expressed. Think of the Genius Move as a meta-tool, one that makes all your other tools work better.

The rest of the book will show you how to apply the Genius Move to accomplish two major goals: ending your specific type of negative thinking and increasing the flow of your authentic creativity. You'll see how to use the tool in your close relationships, your business dealings, your health, and other important areas of life.

In *The Big Leap* we opened up a conversation on discovering your own inner genius. In *The Genius Zone,* we take the conversation to a new level; here you will find out how to live your whole life in the boundless realm of your genius.

The question I want you to consider throughout the book is this: How can I spend the majority of my time doing what I most love to do while making my greatest contribution to the world?

This question is a premier example of what I call a *wonder-question*. A wonder-question is something you sincerely, deeply want to know. It evokes genuine wonder in you. It's such a big and essential question that the answer to it would change your life.

## Experiential Pause

Pause right now to savor the question. Wonder to yourself: Hmmm, how can I spend the majority of my time doing what I most love to do while also making my greatest contribution to the world?

Ask it a few times in your mind to get the feel of it.

As you repeat the wonder-question in your mind, notice the vibrational sound of the words as well as the meaning.

After you say it a few times in your mind, say the question out loud a few times, complete with a hum: Hmmm, how can I spend the majority of my time doing what I most love to do, while also making my greatest contribution to the world?

My own research into this question led me to an unexpected conclusion: our ability to live in our Genius Zone full-time depends on our skill with the meta-tool you will soon learn, the lightning-quick action I call the Genius Move. Once you learn the Genius Move and how to apply it on the fly, you have a practice that can work genuine magic in your life. Even though I have used it thousands of times in my own life and have taught it to thousands of others, the simple power of the practice still fills me with awe when I see it in action.

## The Genius Zone

As your skill with the Genius Move grows, you enter the new dimension we're mapping out: the Genius Zone.

Ultimately, you will come to see that the Genius Zone has no upper limits: it's a spiral. The Genius Spiral is an ascending path that takes you into higher and more productive refinements of your creative expression. As you get nimble at applying the Genius Move in your life, you will likely discover the same joyful secret I did: after you live in the Genius Zone awhile, the Genius Zone lives in you. Your genius wakes up every day before you do.

That's what I want for you. I want you to feel the joy of living in your Genius Zone all the time. I want you to feel the soaring exhilaration of the Genius Spiral every moment of every day. I want you to go through every moment of your life with the deep sense of satisfaction that comes from bringing forth your true creative gifts. If that's what you'd like, too, let's take the first essential step.

## Important Recommendation

You will see activities throughout this book designated as "Hands-On." The best way to master the material is to pause and do the Hands-On Activities on the spot when you encounter them. For example, if I invite you to pause from your reading and write something out in longhand on a piece of paper, please stop reading and do it then and there. Doing the Hands-On Activities as you move along produces the mind-body integration necessary to master the use of the tools.

# 1

## THE ESSENTIAL FIRST STEP

I f you embrace the ideas in the book and follow through with a bit of dedicated practice, you will likely notice two striking results. Both of those results can create revolutionary positive changes in your overall well-being.

The first thing you will likely notice is a sharp decrease in your habitual negative thinking. That's a great boon to your inner harmony, but the second result is even more important. As you turn off the background noise of habitual negative thinking, you open up space for the emergence of new forms of creativity. You make room for your genius.

## Genius and Love

Your genius is discovered by looking closely into what you most love to do. Whether it's writing a poem or sailing a boat or cuddling a newborn, if you love to do it, it's got the essence of your genius in it.

Your genius is the way you go about doing those things you most love to do. When you are living in your Genius Zone, you bring a certain quality of attention to whatever you're doing. You pay attention in a way that's different from when you're doing things you're merely good at.

To use a personal example, I love what I'm doing right now. I love the act of writing and have as long as I can remember. As I sit here, just past six in the morning, doing what you would find me doing almost always at this time of day, I feel a sense of calm exhilaration and deep satisfaction. That feeling is an essential nutrient in my life, and I feel incredibly grateful that I get to feel it every day. It's what originally inspired me to write *The Big Leap*. Once I found my own genius and created my life around it, I felt compelled to share the possibility, first with my clients and later in the book.

The human quest to contact and express our genius often takes us on a journey with many twists and turns. I'd like to share a key conversation at the beginning of my career that set me forth on such a journey. It documents the unpredictable ways that genius often reveals itself.

I already knew I wanted to be a writer by the time I got to college. My dream, like that of thousands of other English majors, was to write the Great American Novel. In those days, though, newspapers were the main place writers found work, so I set my sights on getting a newspaper job until I could get my novel written. All went according to plan, and the year I turned twenty-two I went to work for a newspaper and also began to work on my first book, a novel about a rock star who was coming unglued. However, after only two weeks as a newspaper reporter I hit a major snag: I realized I hated the job. I found it excruciating to sit through a three-hour meeting of the local fish and game commission in order to write a story that would get whittled down to two paragraphs in the paper.

I encountered a different snag with my novel. About a hundred pages into it, I came to the sad conclusion that I didn't yet possess the skills to write even a halfway decent novel, much less the Great American one. So, I quit the newspaper job, put my novel aside, and got a teaching job at a school for juvenile delinquents.

A few weeks after starting my new job, destiny intervened in the form of a suggestion by a gifted teacher, Dr. Dwight Webb. I attended one of Dr. Webb's counseling classes at the University of New Hampshire, as the guest of a friend who was working on his master's degree. The two hours of that class turned my world upside down. More accurately, it turned it right side up.

What I experienced in the counseling class was completely different from any educational experience I'd ever had. Instead of being presented in a lecture format, the class was organized into small groups of about half a dozen people. Our first assignment was to take turns talking for fifteen minutes about something significant that was going on in our lives, while the others in the group focused on listening nonjudgmentally to what was being said. At the end of each person's allotted time, the listeners were simply to offer a brief summary and ask if they'd heard the speaker accurately. We were invited to pay attention to urges we had to criticize, evaluate, or judge what the speaker was saying but not to make any such comments.

The task sounded easy, but it turned out to be maddeningly difficult for me. As I tried listening nonjudgmentally to one person after another, I realized to my great surprise that my head was jam-packed with judgments. As soon as people opened their mouths, my mind started critiquing their voice, personality, appearance, and whatever else I could come up with. The insight jolted me; I saw that most of the time I was not just listening to people, but I was listening to find fault with them.

Then it came my turn to talk about something significant for fifteen minutes. My mouth dry with anxiety, I stumbled through a superficial description of my daily life, not mentioning anything meaningful, such as the fact that I hated practically everything in my life: my job, my apartment, and the body I lived in—which at the time was overweight by more than a hundred pounds and addicted to two packs of Marlboros a day. To top it all off, I had recently gotten married and was already realizing I had made a terrible mistake.

In short, I was ripe for some serious life changes.

I've seen a quotation chiseled in stone on the front of libraries: THE TRUTH SHALL SET YE FREE. To be completely accurate it should probably come with another verse, something like, "but first it shall keep ye up all night." I couldn't sleep for a week after the class. Night after night I replayed the class in my mind, thinking of all the things I could have shared with that group of nonjudgmental strangers. Those sleepless nights drove me to a sad conclusion: I had structured my life around hiding who I really was rather than bringing the real me forth.

Finally, I worked up the courage to enroll in the class and join the counseling program. After class one day I talked to Dr. Webb about a dilemma I couldn't sort out. I told him about my passion for writing and my newfound enthusiasm for human transformation. Should I pursue my writing dreams or put my energy into a career in the counseling field?

He said, "Why not combine the two? Put all your powers of creative writing into real-life things that go on in the counseling process. Nobody's really done that."

His suggestion nudged me out of my either-or thinking and brought forth an outpouring of creativity. Over the next month, I wrote twenty or so poems and prose pieces about the process of counseling. I submitted the poems to a counseling journal, and six months later I got the thrill of seeing my first professional publication in print.

Being in the counseling program helped me experience a magical flip in my attitude toward my job, too. It was stressful work, teaching English and psychology to a hundred kids from rough backgrounds during the school day, then riding herd on them at night as the resident counselor in the dormitories. One of the reasons I'd taken the job was because it came with a rent-free apartment. I'd overlooked the fine print, which said that the apartment was attached to a dormitory that housed twenty-four juvenile delinquents. It was my responsibility to keep the peace in the evening and overnight, a task that involved breaking up fights, combing the hills for runaways, and other activities not conducive to a good night's sleep.

Once I became interested in counseling, I realized I had an abundance of opportunities to apply my new-found skills, such as listening with empathy and sharing honest feelings. As I tapped into more depths of myself—particularly feelings I'd never acknowledged, such as fear, anger, and sadness—I could perceive greater depths of my students' emotional worlds. I began weaving my counseling skills into my teaching and found that it worked wonders. I realized that all of us, even the most belligerent teenager from the harshest background, liked to be listened to nonjudgmentally and spoken to with honesty.

After a while, my attitude toward the job changed completely. Instead of thinking of myself as a glorified prison guard, I saw myself as head monk in a monastery of unruly monks in training. Rather than feeling like a headache-inducing chore, my job took on a new aura: a continuous opportunity to practice counseling skills and grow as a human being at the same time.

Over the next year or so, profound changes came rapidly in every area of my life. In addition to losing a hundred pounds, quitting smoking, and getting out of a painful relationship, I also discovered a new source of creativity deep within me. It was a different kind of creativity from any other I had ever experienced. It was what I now call "true creativity."

## Ordinary Creativity and True Creativity

I make a distinction between ordinary creativity and true creativity. Ordinary creativity is when you use your creative gifts to serve others but not yourself. For example, many of us have had the experience of using our creativity to survive being stuck in a stultifying job. One of my clients, a world-class chemist, worked for a giant food corporation but felt like the lucrative job was killing him. When I asked him what he actually did in his job, he told me he spent his days "researching ways to make salt, sugar and fat more addictive." He yearned for a better use of his skills; his hero was Jonas Salk, the developer of the polio vaccine. Instead of serving humanity, though, my client spent his days figuring out how to get people to eat more potato chips.

True creativity is when your genius serves you and others at the same time. True creativity is when you spend your life doing what you most love to do, in a way that inspires others to do what they most love to do. In my experience, that's living at its very best.

I believe that tapping into our genius is also a key to overall health. One of my favorite quotations comes from the Gospel of Thomas, one of the Apocryphal Gospels edited out of the official Bible: "If you bring forth what is within you, what you bring forth will save you. If you do not bring forth what is within you, what you do not bring forth will destroy you."

I've witnessed the truth of that saying in real life more times than I can count. One of the greatest joys of my life is being with people as they connect with their innate genius and soar off to success in their chosen endeavor. However, I've also seen the negative side of the saying, when people fail to bring forth their true genius. I've felt the pain of being unable to help people I care about, some in my own extended family, from succumbing to addictions and other problems before they could tap their true potential.

## Good Fortune Chases Genius

I began thinking about these matters around 1970 and haven't stopped thinking about them in the half century since. When I first caught sight of the ideas I'm writing about in this book, I had the sobering realization that I wasn't even spending a tiny percentage of my time living in my genius.

By 1975, I finally had enough of my genius "on line" to set a formal goal. I made a vow to spend at least 30 percent of my waking hours in genius-related activities. I chose that number because I could do it without cutting into my job as a professor. To my surprise, I achieved that goal in a year or so, which inspired me to set a new goal of 50 percent. That one took me a few years to attain, because my academic job required me to attend numerous lengthy meetings about subjects of little consequence, including the never-ending issue that surfaced in most faculty meetings: the woeful shortage of faculty parking.

It took me a few years to work my way up to spending half my time in my genius, but after I attained it I took the bold leap of bumping my goal up to 70 percent. Shortly after I made that commitment, an angel swooped into our lives in the person of Oprah Winfrey. In the early '90s, Katie and I made our first journey to Chicago to appear on her show, resulting in our book, *Conscious Loving*, jumping onto the bestseller charts. This happy occurrence allowed us the freedom to spend even more time in our Genius Zones.

Because of those experiences, I've come to believe that good fortune chases the expression of genius. In other words, the more you engage with your genius, the luckier you get. I'm still trying to figure out how that phenomenon works, but I've seen so many examples of it now in my own life and the people I work with that it's made a believer out of me.

To this day I've remained focused on spending more

and more time doing what I most love to do. I estimate that for the past twenty years I've spent 90 percent of my waking hours in genius-related activities. Some things I do, such as loading the dishwasher or tidying up the kitty litter, don't call forth my genius, but I enjoy doing them because they contribute to overall well-being. Most of the time, though, I get to do what I'm doing right now, and I love it.

I want everybody everywhere to have the opportunity to discover and express their genius. That may seem like an outrageously unattainable goal, but I am confident it will eventually catch on. I base my confidence on one simple bedrock fact: *living in your Genius Zone feels absolutely wonderful!* Once you feel that special kind of wonderfulness, I predict you won't ever want to live anywhere else.

Think of the allover satisfaction you feel when you eat the perfect amount of a food you love. Think of the sweet body sensations you feel when you wake up after a good night of sleep and give yourself a big stretch. In my experience, the whole-body joy of living in the Genius Zone is just like that. I can't help but think it's bound to catch on.

You and I may not be around to witness the full

flowering of an entire humanity living in genius. However, we have a great advantage of our own. We get to be here *now*, in the pioneering stage of liberating the full genius of our species. Imagine the awe that pioneers in their horse-drawn wagons must have felt when they saw the Rocky Mountains for the first time! That's the same kind of opportunity we have now. We get to experience the wonder of opening up new territory in the human quest to realize our full potential.

## The Crucial Step

Many of you have had the experience of being on a team. I have a mix of painful and exhilarating feelings on the subject myself. In elementary school, I was the fat kid who always got picked last for any team sport. I can still feel the burning humiliation of standing there while every other kid got picked before me. By high school, though, I had grown some muscle and shot up to 6′1″ in height, becoming a burly 225-pounder rather than a flabby fat boy. In spite of a nearly total absence of athletic skill, my size got me a place as a backup lineman on the football team.

I spent most of my time on the bench, but there's one moment I remember as if it were yesterday. In the seventh game of the season, Coach Whitey Perkins looked over at me on the bench and jerked his chin toward the field. "Hendricks, you're in."

What I learned in that moment has stuck with me all my life: there's an unmeasurable distance between being on the bench and being on the field.

One moment I was on the bench, and the next moment I was on the field for the first time in a real game. The feeling was completely different. On the bench, all my potential was inside me, fully contained. As I ran onto the field, I felt like my feet were barely touching the ground. It was exhilarating, but also scary, because my potential was now real and on display for all to see.

Time spent on the bench is theoretical, based on what we think we might do if we were in the game. The moment you get on the field you enter a new domain, one that has an entry ticket with a unique paradox of a price: you can only buy in with something that costs nothing but requires everything.

Commitment is what we're talking about.

It took me a long time to learn a simple truth about life: all successful self-change begins with heartfelt commitment. In other words, we get what we're *committed* to getting out of life. That goes two ways, however.

We get the positive things we're committing to getting, but you may find, as I did, that you have unconscious commitments that cause you to keep doing things that hurt you.

For example, after a number of relationship disasters in my teens and twenties, I discovered I had an unconscious commitment to being criticized, lied to, and ultimately abandoned by women. I feel embarrassed that it took me until I was nearly thirty to figure all that out; it's something a Psych 101 student could have pointed out in two minutes if I'd been willing to listen, which I wasn't much in those days.

Here's the background. Like many of you, I had a rough start to my life. A few weeks after conceiving me, my father died at age thirty-two under mysterious circumstances. It's unclear whether he died suddenly of a rare disease or had a hand in his own demise. A few months later it finally dawned on my mother that not only had she been left behind with a six-year-old son, three hundred dollars, and a car that wasn't paid for, she was also pregnant. The stress of this cataclysm caused her addictions to get out of control. Chaos ensued, and it wasn't until I was handed off at birth to a loving grandmother that things stabilized.

Roll the clock forward to my midtwenties, when I found myself mindlessly repeating a similar pattern in my relationships with women—no matter whether they hailed from Florida or Michigan or Maine, the women I took up with all had several things in common: they were all quick to blame me for everything that was wrong in their lives, they had secret addictions I didn't know about, and they ultimately departed in ways that left me mystified.

With utter obliviousness to the origins of the pattern, I unconsciously managed to turn the painful drama of my early life into a series of recycling relationship cataclysms. Almost fifty years after that wake-up moment, I can still feel the power of that discovery: it wasn't the women—it was me! I was the source of the bad luck with women I'd been complaining about!

Even after decades of experience with many clients, I am still moved by how much the early days of our lives affect our relationships and total well-being. It is also humbling to see how even the smartest people can be utterly oblivious to how these early patterns are creating misery in their lives today. Speaking as a recovering oblivious smart person, I still find it hard to believe I could have once been so thickheaded that I overlooked the real forces that were driving me through half a dozen broken relationships in my teens and twenties.

What finally enabled me to wake up from that recurring bad dream was a heartfelt commitment I made to a new kind of relationship I'd never known or seen. Once I made that commitment, it took only one month for my dream mate to show up in real life.

## Heartfelt Commitment Is the Key

Your mind can conceive of a magnificent positive future for you, but your heart is what will make it real. When you get your heart's energy behind a positive goal your mind has chosen, you are virtually unstoppable. I want to show you how to use a specific type of commitment to accomplish two very specific goals: ending your negative thinking and giving a quantum boost to your own unique creativity.

### HANDS-ON ACTIVITY

Get paper and a favorite writing implement. You may want to use a notebook, so you can keep all your Hands-On Activities in one place.

In your own handwriting, write out the following sentence three times, filling in the blank with your name. Write this in bigger, bolder letters than you ordinarily use, as if you're making a BIG statement:

**I, _____, commit to ending my negative thinking and liberating my true creativity.**

Notice your breathing as you write the sentences out. Does it slow down? Speed up? Does it shift locations in your body? Simply take note of your breathing, like you might notice what the speedometer on a car is telling you.

When you have finished writing out the commitment three times, pause for a moment of self-assessment. Does this feel like a commitment you really want to make? Is it sincere and heartfelt? If so, proceed along to the next section. If not, explore what might be in the way of making a heartfelt commitment. Don't proceed to chapter 2 until you feel a sincere commitment to ending negative thinking and liberating your authentic creativity.

## Recommitment

Committing gets you into the game, but recommitting is what gets you to the goal. Most of us don't get to our goals without stumbling, tripping, and wandering off track a few times along the way. Recommitting keeps you out of the trap of criticizing yourself for wandering off track. When you notice you've strayed from the path to your goal, recommitting gets you oriented correctly again.

Commitment is like the moment you jump from the side of the pool into the water. In contrast to being a spectator in your life, committing gets you into the action. Just as with swimming, you don't know what you need to learn to succeed until you get in the pool. You might have natural abilities or qualities that you don't discover until you actually get in the pool or on the field.

Committing gets the process started, but it's how you encounter the obstacles that inevitably arise that determines the success of the journey. Unless you're astonishingly lucky, you're going to encounter obstacles on your way to a goal. You'll come up against your beliefs about getting from here to there. You'll get distracted by one thing or the other, and judgments will surface along with old memories and your own unfaced fears.

When I first began my own journey of transformation, I had a view of commitment as a onetime event. After a while, though, I realized it was really an ongoing process of encountering obstacles, getting thrown off track, then recommitting and getting back on the path again.

Recommitment gets you out of all-or-nothing thinking that causes minor slips to turn into epic detours of self-sabotage. A friend, now with two decades of sobriety, gave me a vivid example: "I got sober the first

time when I was around thirty. After two years of sobriety I had a slip. I took a sip of white wine at a party.
I could have gone to a meeting, confessed my slip, and
recommitted, but instead I thought to myself, 'Since
I took one sip, I might as well just finish the glass—it
would be a shame to waste it.' I finished the glass and
then two bottles more, and there went the next eleven
years of my life. I didn't get sober again until I was
forty-three."

That's why we need to factor in recommitting as a
key part of the process. It makes the journey much
more pleasurable if you don't hold yourself to a perfect
standard. Your goals are like setting the destination on
an airplane's autopilot. By the time the plane gets from
New York to Honolulu, it's made thousands of tiny corrections to keep nudging the plane back on track after
it's slipped off. In fact, the plane gets all the way from
New York to a tiny speck of land in the middle of the
ocean by being off track most of the time.

The secret is recommitting. Each time the plane goes
slightly off track, the autopilot notices it and recom-
mits to the goal. If only we humans were as good at
receiving feedback as an autopilot! In my early days I
used to get so attached to being right that I would re-

ject opportunities to make corrections in time to avoid disasters.

When you learn how to recommit, you open up the possibility of enjoying the pleasures of the journey. If you know you're likely to get off track occasionally and have developed the skill of recommitting, you simply focus again on what you really want and take a concrete action, even a small one, that takes you toward the goal. Before I figured that out, I would often get so focused on arriving at the goal that I forgot to savor the journey along the way.

Beating up on yourself—with shame, blame, and criticism for getting off track—is one of the common traps. Blaming yourself for wandering off the path just slows you down. All that's required is a simple moment of awareness: "Oops, slipped off my chosen path. Time to recommit." Awareness is important; criticism is absolutely unnecessary.

Those of you, like me, who have a perfectionist streak in your personality may find it challenging to give up self-criticism and replace it with the friendlier process of self-awareness and recommitment. I was well into my third decade of life before I became aware of how much criticism and blame I aimed at myself.

As I focused more on this issue, I came to realize that self-blame and criticism were actually addictions.

The quick way to find out if you're addicted to something is to stop it and see what happens. As I took my first steps in loving and appreciating myself instead of blaming and criticizing, I found that my new commitment was good for about ten seconds. I'd feel a moment of liberation, then my old habit of self-criticism would kick back in. That's why I began to regard it as an addiction. But what was driving it all? What was I really addicted to?

The answer, when it finally revealed itself to me, set me back on my heels. I realized I was addicted to suffering! Later, I came across a quotation from the teacher and philosopher G. I. Gurdjieff: "It is very difficult also to sacrifice one's suffering. A man will renounce any pleasures you like but he will not give up his suffering." I could feel the truth of that in my bones, and it inspired me to find out if I could give up my own addiction to suffering.

That's how I first discovered the concept I described in *The Big Leap*, what I call the *Upper Limit Problem*. (Students in our programs humorously refer to it as "ULP," rhyming with "gulp.") When I was attempting to kick my addiction to self-criticism, I found that I began to maintain a sense of loving acceptance of myself for longer and longer periods of time. Eventually, though, I'd have an ULP. Whether it was after ten minutes of good feeling or ten days, I'd finally do something that sabotaged the flow of well-being I was experiencing. I'd have an argument with my girlfriend or crack a rib falling off my bike or run out of gas on the freeway (all three of those being personal ULPs of mine). Then I'd be back to beating myself up again.

I hope you're not as thickheaded as I was in those days. There were some stubborn issues in myself that took dozens of recommitments to clear them up. For example, I mentioned earlier that I struggled with weight for the first twenty-four years of my life. I resembled the Pillsbury Doughboy as a baby, but an extra hundred pounds on an adult is not as cute. Finally I woke up in my twenties and committed to create a new body. After I made the commitment, though, I discovered that the real magic lay in recommitment.

My self-devised diet was simple: I ate only foods I'd never eaten before. I reasoned that everything I'd ever eaten up until then contributed to being a hundred pounds overweight, so a simple solution was to eat new things. During my year of radical and rapid weight loss, I discovered the delights of never-before-tasted foods such as broccoli, asparagus, artichokes, and smoked salmon. The diet worked fabulously well, so well, in fact, that I also encountered dozens of what I would later call Upper Limit Problems.

I lost five pounds in the first few days of eating the new way, then my first ULP kicked in. I got an intense craving for peanut butter, one of my main staple foods since my early days as a latchkey kid. It was definitely in the category of "things I'd eaten before," but I broke my vow and ate half a jar. The next day I'd gained back two of my precious five lost pounds. I continued going back and forth between success and sabotage, with many recommitments along the way, losing 35 to 40 pounds in the process. I was feeling great, so great that I hit an uber-ULP one day walking past an ice cream shop. I saw a family eating a giant banana split, and almost as if in a trance, I went in and ordered one for myself. Twenty minutes later I staggered out of the shop in a delirium of satisfaction and guilt. A half hour after that, though, I learned a lasting lesson: I got the worst stomachache of my life. It was so memorable, it cured me of my self-sabotage programming with my weight. After my banana split experience, I noticed my Upper Limit cravings but didn't indulge in them. As a result, I lost the rest of my sixty-five extra pounds with only a few minor detours.

As you can probably tell by now, I'm a cheerleader for the act of recommitting. If any of you suffer as I did from the habit of punishing yourself when you break commitments, I implore you as you go along through the book to loosen your grip on that habit. Use this book as a breakthrough opportunity to love yourself for all your flaws, foibles, and failings. By loving them, you avoid the costly and time-consuming trap of self-blame. You free up more energy to recommit to your goals.

# Interlude

## Breathing, Emotions,
## and Your Personal Growth

You will notice I refer often to breathing as we do Hands-On Activities. If you're new to the use of breathing for transformation, I think you'll grow to find it an extremely useful tool and a good friend, both in this book and in life in general. It's a natural resource, free and always available. I've used breathwork in all my seminars for forty-some years now. Based on that experience, I have great confidence in the power of breathing to speed up and deepen learning about yourself, particularly in the area of your emotions.

Your breathing has been refined over millions of

years to reflect your emotional state. Just like our cave-dwelling ancestors of fifty thousand years ago, if you are out for a stroll in the woods and see a grizzly bear coming in your direction, your brain will perceive a possible threat and administer a shot of adrenaline to your bloodstream. Within a split second, your muscles tighten, your heart pumps faster, your breathing quickens and shifts up higher in your chest. In the twitch of an eye your body is prepared for the Four Fs: fight, flee, freeze, or faint.

If you're like most of us, you will choose the flee option rather than charging the grizzly bear. If you're a rabbit or a possum, you might go with the freeze or faint option, choosing to stay motionless or roll up into a ball until the danger passes.

Fortunately, most of us aren't required to deal with actual bears on a regular basis anymore. On the other hand, if wild animals were all we had to deal with, modern life would be luxurious indeed. Our modern lives have stresses our cave-person ancestors never had to deal with. Foul air, food drenched in chemicals, the din of traffic, the background chant of alarming news—these are the grizzlies we face every day. Our bodies respond to these modern stresses with the same internal wiring inherited from our days of fending off sabertooth tigers and club-wielding neighbors.

BACK TO THE BREATH

Since we can't change a few million years of evolution overnight, we need to know how to handle the ancient feelings that still come forth, often in ways that trouble us. Particularly, awareness of your breathing can really assist you with issues related to fear, anger, sexual attraction, and grief. With a bit of practice, you can turn your ancient feelings into a source of power.

Here's an example of how you can creatively use your breathing in a stressful situation. I worked for one session with a man I'll call Maury. In that session, he learned something he credits with giving a life-changing boost to his happiness and overall well-being. Here's what happened:

He came in as a referral from a local psychologist who had read about some of my work with breathing and anxiety. Maury gave me a few minutes of detail about his job and how his anxiety was blocking his advancement, but it took only about ten seconds to see what the real problem was. He held his breath against his feelings.

I noticed right away that when he talked about his anxiety, he would tighten his belly muscles and push his breathing up into his chest. It's one of the most common problems that besets us as humans. We often have ancient feelings stirring in us, but the expression of those feelings is frowned upon in modern society. If you're getting berated by your boss, you may have the urge to pummel him with a cudgel or run screaming from the room, but most of us learn at an early age to curtail those impulses and stuff them away.

Your breathing sits in the middle of this eternal struggle, the conflict between how you actually feel and how you must pretend to feel in order to get by in whatever social situation you're in. Your breathing is run by both your ancient autonomic nervous system and the conscious thinking machinery in your modern cortex. You can easily verify this: you can consciously choose to take a big breath, but you can also forget about your breathing for hours at a time and it will do just fine on its own. For that reason, your breathing is perfectly positioned as an intermediary between your conscious and unconscious minds.

I showed Maury how he was fighting to control his anxiety by restricting his breath and tensing muscles in the belly area where our biggest sensations of fear live. I explained how he was trying to push his rising anxiety back down into his belly by turning his breathing upside down. With a normal, healthy breath, we relax our belly muscles and allow the in breath to go all the way to fullness. Maury was doing the exact opposite. Attempting to shut out his anxiety, he tightened his belly muscles when he breathed in, preventing him from ever getting a full breath.

With an hour of coaching, Maury got his breath right side up. He breathed with his anxiety instead of against it, allowing himself to feel the emotion instead of trying to pretend it wasn't there. Breath is designed to flow with our emotions, not to be used as a weapon against them. The moment we figure this out, the body rewards us with rushes of good feelings where the anxiety used to be.

Here's one more practical nugget that can really improve your life. Your breathing has a different pace and quality for the different feelings human beings commonly have. If you turn the searchlight of awareness on your breathing, you have a clear window into the feelings and sensations that are attempting to deliver you important information.

The sensations that compose the feeling of anger are trying to tell you that somehow your boundaries are being violated. For example, a primly dressed professional woman consulted me a few years back about chronic pain. She was a vice president at a large bank, managing a dozen or so people under her. She had a house, a husband, two children, and a career on the ascendance, but she couldn't enjoy any of this because her life was plagued by headaches.

Joan, as I'll call her, was also literally getting sick and

tired of the medications she'd been prescribed for her headaches. She said they made her feel fatigued all day and also made her feel in her stomach like she was on the edge of nausea. She wanted to find a more natural way of dealing with her headaches.

I was intrigued when I heard her describe one of the side effects she was attributing to the drug: "on the edge of nausea." That's nearly exactly the same phrase I use with clients to coach them on the emotion of fear. I ask them to pay attention to an edge-of-nausea sensation, a slight queasiness in the stomach. When those sensations are there, we're usually scared about something.

Your mind doesn't care if you're making up your fears in your head or there is actually something threatening in your physical environment. Its job is to tell you when you're feeling fear. Your body is busily sending up signals to start doing one or more of the Four Fs: flee, fight, freeze, or faint. The cat zips away from the dog, the dog snarls at the postman, the deer freezes in the headlights, the sloth rolls up and sleeps. The human version goes like this: Some people shy away from confrontations (flee), others use their anger to scare everyone around them (fight). A third group seizes up and gets confused in the face of conflict (freeze), while a fourth group yawns and spaces out (faint).

Specifically, when the body is sending fear signals up to the mind, it is saying, "I'm revving up down here. There's some sort of problem going on. I'm not sure what it is, but I'm ready to go."

Two situations often triggered Joan's headaches. Being criticized was one; the other was being asked to do something she felt was unfair, such as when the bank president would storm in at five minutes before closing with some urgent problem she needed to handle.

I spent an hour helping her learn how to use her breath awareness to banish her headaches. Here's what I showed her: when we're scared, the way we breathe looks and feels different from when we're angry or sad. You can check this out for yourself. Notice that when you get scared, your belly muscles tighten and your breath shifts up higher in your chest.

If I had to pick one aspect of breathing to focus on, one that would have the greatest payoff in health and happiness, it would be to notice when your breathing shifts up into your chest. It does that when you're angry and when you're scared. The important thing to remember is that when we get angry about something, we're usually scared, too. Look for those two feelings to occur in tandem.

Next time you notice your belly muscles tighten and your breathing shift up into your chest, ask yourself the following:

What am I angry about?

What am I scared about?

From a practical standpoint, it is incredibly important to explore the fear that is usually hidden underneath whatever we're angry about. The reason it is so important is that when you can name and acknowledge the fear beneath your anger, you can get to the source of the energy that has been causing your anger to recycle.

After a few sessions, Joan built up enough confidence in her ability to name and express her feelings that she was able to speak to her boss effectively. One afternoon he asked her to stay after closing time to handle some piece of business. Instead of keeping her feelings stuffed inside, she told him that she got angry and scared when he made such requests. She said it put her in a bind because she was scared to displease him and also scared that she wouldn't pick up her son from soccer practice on time and get home to cook dinner for the family. To her amazement, her boss didn't get angry with her for communicating so honestly. Quite the opposite, in fact. He apologized and invited her to let him know about other things he did that stimulated her anger and fear. Not surprisingly, the frequency of her headaches declined rapidly after the conversation and faded away completely after a few months.

## SUMMARIZING

Based on my experiences with breathing, both in my own life and with my clients, I've become a passionate advocate for the therapeutic and transformational use of breathing. It's one of my life's passions to help as many people as possible discover the power of this natural resource and put it to work for themselves. Breath awareness has changed my own life profoundly; it's my hope that it will have as important an effect on yours.

# 2

## MASTERING THE GENIUS MOVE

Now, take a few generous breaths of loving acceptance for yourself, open your mind wide with wonder, and consider a piece of wisdom it took me half a lifetime to figure out: Anytime you are unhappy, you are thinking about something you cannot possibly change or control. Unhappiness comes from trying to control things that are actually uncontrollable and trying to change things that are actually unchangeable.

Here's another way to say it: When you focus on things you have no power to change, you get unhappy.

When you focus on things you actually have the power to change, you get happy.

For example, back when I was fat, I made myself miserable by obsessing constantly about how much I weighed, often getting on the scale several times a day. It was a huge wake-up moment for me when I first realized that I had absolutely no control over how much I weighed. I could stand on the scale for an hour and it wouldn't budge.

Through using the Genius Move, though, I quit obsessing about my weight and put my attention only on things that had the power to make a difference with my weight. Instead of worrying about my weight, I developed a much more useful obsession: paying close attention to what I put in my mouth and the amount of exercise I got every day. I started asking with every food I considered eating, "Will this feed the new body I'm creating or my old body?" Ultimately, I made the question even simpler: "Will this food feed my spirit?"

This question led me to start eating apples instead of candy bars, green vegetables instead of french fries, blueberries instead of ice cream. I began taking a brisk walk after lunch rather than a nap. A year later I was more than a hundred pounds lighter.

In that year of radical life change, I learned a great deal about the Genius Moment and the Genius Move. I discovered that we get many Genius Moments throughout the day, each one a gateway to the Genius Zone.

## The Genius Moment Close-up

The Genius Moment begins when you notice you feel unhappy in some way and go in search of what you are trying to control that's actually uncontrollable. For example, the Genius Moment is when you notice your shoulders are tense and realize that you are working hard trying to change someone who does not want to change. The Genius Move is when you let go of your effort to control the uncontrollable and feel the new space of creative aliveness open up inside you.

You have probably discovered, as I have, that sometimes the person who doesn't want to change is standing right in front of you . . . looking back at you from the mirror. There have been times in my life when I've been so stubbornly unwilling to look at my own patterns that my resistance has compelled me to repeat them over and over until something has come along to snap me out of the trance.

I'd like to tell you about one particular moment of

snapping out of a painful trance, thanks to the Genius Move. See if you can relate. Have you ever sat home alone on a Saturday night, wishing you were not sitting home alone on a Saturday night? If you've experienced something like that, you're definitely not alone. One particular lonely night helped me learn the power of spotting a Genius Moment and applying the Genius Move.

Up until I was twenty-nine, I thought falling in love mostly happened in movies and corny love songs, maybe was even just an invention of the greeting card industry to hawk their products. Then, suddenly, I had to junk all my prior assumptions about the subject. I fell in love.

I had all the classic symptoms. I found myself thinking about Karen all the time, even when I was trying to think about other things, such as doing my job. Whenever I thought of her I had thrills of bliss that flowed up from my belly and played in my throat. Sometimes my thoughts would turn negative; in the wake of those sour thoughts would come waves of anxiety, especially when I would think of her with another man. Not just any man—her former boyfriend.

When I first met Karen, we had a six-week period of

uninterrupted, ecstatic connection, and I think part of me just assumed that this exalted feeling would go on forever. Then, one day she announced she was going back to Wisconsin for a week. Since Wisconsin was where her former boyfriend lived, I was inspired to poke my nose in where it definitely didn't belong. I asked her, "Do you plan to see Gary?"

First, Karen vigorously reminded me it was none of my business, but then she relented and told me that, in fact, she had already made plans to spend the coming weekend with Gary. Ouch! I suddenly wished I hadn't asked. I was forced to consider the possibility that Karen wasn't as much in love with me as I was with her.

Roll the clock forward to Saturday night of that weekend. There I sat, slumped on the same couch where she and I had cuddled just a couple of nights before. Now I sat on it by myself, feeling more miserable than I could ever remember.

Suddenly, though, in the depths of my gloom a ray of light appeared with a new insight: I was a research-trained psychologist! I could turn the experience into an experiment! Since I'd never felt quite this miserable, I was in a perfect place to learn something big from it. If I could figure out how to get out of this rock-bottom low, I would have a skill that could help me face other difficult things that were bound to come my way in life. Maybe I could also learn something that would be useful for working with clients.

Sitting there on the couch, I went in search of what actually could have been causing me to feel so unhappy. I saw a thought flit through my mind of Karen with Gary, picturing them making joyous love on that same Saturday night I was feeling so unloved. I went in search of the source of that thought, and there it was: I was trying to control Karen's feelings and what she did with her life. I was particularly trying to control her sexual attractions, which I definitely had no power to control.

Above all, I also realized I'd been trying to control my own feelings of sadness, fear, and anger. It occurred to me that all the negative thoughts darting through my head over the past few days—trying to figure out what I'd done to deserve this, wishing I had never met her, picturing myself flying to Wisconsin to rescue her from Gary's clutches—had been attempts by my mind to control my feelings.

The truth dawned on me: I'd been doing that my

whole life! As long as I could remember, I'd been keeping my emotions at bay by using my mind to distract me from them.

With a whoosh of relief, I let go of the effort required to control any aspect of Karen. At the same time, I let go of trying to control my own anger, sadness, and fear. A new sensation coursed through me, as if I'd released the reins of a horse I'd been desperately trying to restrain. The rush of letting go brought with it a mix of relief, ecstasy, and fear.

What was I afraid of? As I tuned in to it, I became aware of the nature of the fear; it was not a specific one, such as fear of snakes or high places, but rather was a generalized fear of the unknown. I had never been aware of it, but there it was down in the center of my belly.

I was gifted then with another Genius Moment. I realized I was trying to control the fear itself, mostly by keeping the muscles in my abdomen squeezed tight. I softened my belly muscles and let go of trying to control the fear sensations. I took a deep breath and let my fear be instead of trying to make it go away.

I was astonished by what happened next. The sensations of fear receded into a faint shimmer and then disappeared, leaving behind a sweet feeling of ease and flow. I took a bigger, relaxed breath and felt the easeful, sweet sensations expand even more.

I came out of my slouch and sat bolt upright on the couch, electrified by the energy of the new awareness yet also feeling deeply at peace. There I was, sitting on the same piece of furniture where I'd sprawled in my misery a few minutes before. Now I felt reborn.

You can probably guess what eventually happened to the relationship. We took a few more spins on the drama-go-round before we finally got off and went our separate ways. It's been more than forty years since I've seen Karen, but I'll always remain grateful to her, first for the experience of falling in love but also for that Saturday night of pain and joy alone on the couch. The relationship ended, but I came away with a gift that still illuminates my present: a new relationship with my own feelings as well as with the people around me.

I feel happiest when I greet my feelings with loving acceptance rather than trying to control them. I feel much happier when I listen to my fears, anger, and sorrow instead of drowning them out by smoking or stuffing myself with food. The same is true for the people in my life. My relationships are happier when I give people space to be who they are, rather than thinking of them as my own personal improvement projects.

## HANDS-ON ACTIVITY

I'd like you to get physical with the life-changing principle we've been exploring. Now it's time to take the idea out of your mind and put it in your body so it can start working miracles for you.

### INSTRUCTIONS

Get the following materials:

**Two file folders**

**Two pieces of paper**

**Two pens: one that writes in red and another that writes in green**

Place your two folders before you. On one, write the following in big, bold letters with your red pen:

### *THINGS I ABSOLUTELY CANNOT CONTROL*

On the other file, write boldly in green:

### *THINGS I ABSOLUTELY CAN CONTROL*

Your instructions will continue in a moment, but first I want to give you two examples to start your file, using common unproductive obsessions most of us struggle with at some point in our lives. The first example is one I certainly can relate to from my own experience. See if you can, too.

## The First Unproductive Obsession

Many people waste a great deal of their time and mental energy being concerned about what other people think of them. They manufacture mental images of other people criticizing them for such things as their looks, their intelligence, and their actions. They get occasional pats on the back from these imaginary people, too, but, in general, they experience a nagging harangue of negativity ricocheting around in the cramped space between their ears.

What a relief, then, to come to our senses and realize we have absolutely no control over what other people think of us!

Now, back to your activity.

Take one of your pieces of paper and write the following on it with your red pen in big, bold letters:

PERFORM THE GENIUS MOVE WHEN I THINK ABOUT THESE THINGS

### 1. What other people think about me

Put this piece of paper in your Red File.

The reason it goes in your Red File is that none of us have any control over what any other organism thinks about us. For example, you can train your dog or cat to like you by feeding and petting it every day, but you will never know exactly what it really thinks of you. The dog may regard you as godlike for passing out free food, whereas the cat may think you're a gullible sucker. You will never really know. In the same way, you can never really know what your doctor, your lawyer, your therapist, or your spouse thinks about you. You can certainly never control or change what they think, because they're over there in a separate organism.

It's a life-changing moment when any of us wakes up to that realization, but when we hold up the mirror to ourselves, we see something even more stunning: none of us have control over what *we ourselves* think about other people. No matter how many positive-thinking books we read or seminars we attend, we are never immune to a string of negative thoughts breaking through.

Winston Churchill is sometimes said to have made a wise observation about maturing. He said that when we're twenty, we spend a lot of time worrying about what other people think of us. When we get to forty, we stop worrying so much about what people think of us. When we get to sixty, though, we realize nobody had been thinking of us, anyway.

## The Second Unproductive Obsession

Many of us squander our mental energy thinking about the past. We squander more energy thinking in unproductive ways about the future. Most thoughts about the past and the future are about things we have absolutely no power to change.

When we're thinking about the past, we call to mind long-ago events and sort through them. We interact mentally with long-dead figures, often carrying on arguments with them in our heads and stewing in the emotions churned up by these imaginary conversations. We also replay conversations we've already had, editing our responses for maximum effect.

Self-critical thoughts are a troublesome subset of rumination about the past and future. If you study your self-critical thoughts carefully, you'll notice that many of them are critical comments about things you did in the past. Other self-critical comments are pegged to the future, to things you haven't actually experienced yet. Still other critical thoughts are connected to events in both the past and the future.

For example, perhaps you notice yourself thinking, "What's wrong with me? Why don't I call Mom and Dad more often?" With that thought, you are criticizing yourself for not calling them often enough in the past, while at the same time trying to make yourself call them more in the future by the application of that powerful but painful motivator, guilt.

All this mental and emotional agitation calms down when we feel in our bones the bottom-line truth: Nobody has any control over what happened in the past. It already happened. It's unchangeable.

If it's so obvious that we cannot control such things as the past, the future, and what other people think of us, why do we persist in doing it? The answer is painfully obvious: it's an addiction. As I explored this issue in myself, I gradually came to see that I was addicted to thinking about the past, the future, how other people saw me, and a host of other things I actually had no power to change. Seeing it as an addiction was helpful because that led me to ask myself what the addiction was covering up.

A friend of mine, a recovering alcoholic, told me of a saying he learned in his recovery: "You don't find out what you've been drinking *for* until you stop drinking." The same applies to smoking, drugs, and excessive eating. In other words, there is something deep in you that is being covered over by your addictions, something that your addictions are helping you keep hidden. In the case of alcohol, you have to stop drinking, if only for a day, before you can even begin to understand what's been driving you to drink.

I found this to be true in my own case. Ultimately, I discovered that all my self-destructive habits were an attempt to outrun the fear of my own creativity. I was afraid to surrender fully to the creative life I really wanted to live. I was half-heartedly trying to live an ordinary life, meanwhile keeping myself distracted by eating and smoking myself to death.

## Back to Your Files

When you notice that you're thinking about someone's opinion of you or dwelling on the past or the future, your first task is to stop those thoughts. The best way to stop thinking about things you can't change is to start thinking about things you *can* change.

### INSTRUCTIONS

In your Red File, write "The past" on your paper as the second thing you absolutely cannot change or control.

PERFORM THE GENIUS MOVE WHEN I THINK ABOUT THESE THINGS

1. *What other people think about me*
2. *The past*

Put this piece of paper in your Red File and turn your attention to your Green File.

Take your second piece of paper and write this on it in green:

*THINK ABOUT THESE THINGS INSTEAD*

*THINGS I CAN DO IN THE NEXT TEN MINUTES THAT*
*COULD CONTRIBUTE TO MY OWN HAPPINESS*
*AND THE HAPPINESS OF SOMEONE ELSE*

Examples:

**Pick up the phone, call a friend or family member, and tell them how much I appreciate them.**

**Sit down for a few minutes and write what I'm feeling in my journal.**

**Instead of the past, think about what I want to create right now and take action.**

Examples:

**Convert spare bedroom into exercise room**

**Organize photos for memoir**

**Write a song for wife's birthday**

Pause from your Hands-On Activity and take a deeper look at the future.

## The Future Is Beyond Our Control

Thinking about the future can be one of the best things human beings do. For example, consciously planning for your old age can save a lot of worry time later. The same is true for making travel plans or laying out the pots and pans you'll need for a cooking project. There are many good uses for the future-thinking machinery in your mind. We wouldn't have gotten to where we are as a species without our ability to think about the future.

But . . .

Just like the amazing skills of explaining and justifying, the ability to think about the future makes us miserable when we hitch it to our unconscious needs and feelings.

For example, I've worked with hundreds of people who suffer, as I once did, from a fear of speaking in public. I've often told the story of the man who approached me after my first speech to a professional audience. He gave me a compliment that ricocheted around in my head for quite a while afterward.

He said, "I really enjoyed your talk. It wasn't so much what you said but the way you said it." I beamed all over and asked him what he liked about the way I'd spoken. He said, "I could really relate to you. Your voice shakes just as badly as mine does when I try to speak in public."

My mood fell like a punctured soufflé, but his odd

compliment did me the favor of unleashing a flood of realizations. Later that day, on a plane bound for the Bay Area to give another speech, I spent the bumpy ride trying to figure out what made my voice shake. I was obviously afraid of something, but what was it?

When the ability to think about the future gets hooked to the fear of public speaking, we unconsciously project unpleasant images on our inner mind screen. We go out into the future mentally to imagine the audience booing us or arguing with us or storming for the exits. This horror-movie display of negative thinking occurs in the space between our ears, stirring up fear in our bellies and sadness in our hearts, tensing the anger muscles in the back of our necks.

The first thing that occurred to me was that I had prepared and rehearsed my talk without ever projecting a conscious image of the audience responding positively. In the week before the talk, my unconscious mind sent up dozens of images of the audience booing me, getting bored, going to sleep, and standing up to argue with me, along with a host of other unpleasant pictures. Never once, though, did it occur to me to use the awesome picture-forming ability of the mind to establish positive images of the audience's reactions.

The second realization was life-changing: my voice shook because I was trying to control my fear and hide it from the audience! Out of that insight, a radical idea occurred to me. The next morning, I stepped onstage to give a speech to an audience of about a hundred and fifty teachers and counselors. Instead of trying to hide anything from the audience, I went to the opposite extreme: I told them the story of what had happened the day before in Kansas City. They roared with laughter and later rewarded me with a standing ovation.

According to my notebook from that era, I got paid a hundred and fifty dollars each, plus travel expenses, to give those two speeches. They ultimately turned out to be priceless, because I got a lesson that cured me of the voice shakes and sent me forth to give more than two thousand and five hundred talks, seminars, and media appearances. I realized that all I had to do was speak honestly about what I knew and what was going on with me. All I really needed to focus on was that every word I spoke resonated with my inner experience. I didn't need to control my feelings or how the audience reacted to me.

Back to your Hands-On Activity . . .

### INSTRUCTIONS

In your Red File, write "The future" on your paper as the third thing you absolutely cannot change or control.

PERFORM THE GENIUS MOVE WHEN I THINK ABOUT THESE THINGS

*1. What other people think about me*

*2. The past*

*3. The future*

Put this piece of paper in your Red File and turn your attention to your Green File.

Take your piece of paper and add a positive suggestion in green:

Instead of worrying about the future, make a short list of things I can do in the next ten minutes that could contribute to my own happiness and the happiness of someone else.

## In Your Daily Life

Over the coming days and weeks, be on the lookout for other things you can add to your **Red File** and your **Green File.** The examples I've given apply to almost all of us. However, bigger discoveries await you as you explore your own idiosyncratic and infinite depths. I urge you to go on a joyful but relentless search for all the things you've been trying to control that are actually not yours to control. Replace those fretful, frustrating, and fruitless thoughts with ideas about what you can change right now, and watch the magic reveal itself.

## The Genius Move in Slow Motion

I'd like to explore the Genius Move with you in step-by-step detail. You will eventually learn to execute it in a split second, but for the purposes of learning, let's break it into five steps. Here's the sequence:

1. You notice any sort of unhappiness occurring somewhere in you. Perhaps your shoulders are feeling tight or you are recycling unpleasant thoughts such as what's wrong with you, with others, or the world.

2. You ask yourself, "What am I trying to control that's actually not within my power to control?"

3. Sometimes you get an insight; sometimes you don't. The wondering is the important part of the move, not the insight. Many of your biggest insights about what you're trying to control will come later that day or even in your dreams.

4. Formally declare it outside your control, even if
   you don't have a clear insight about exactly what
   it is. Say in your mind or out loud, "I consciously
   let go of trying to control it, whatever it is." If
   you have an insight about the specific issue, put it
   in the sentence like this: "I consciously let go of
   trying to control whether Jane loves me or not,"
   or, "I consciously let go of trying to control my
   nervousness when I speak in public."

5. Think of a positive action you can do right away,
   something you actually have control over, and take
   the action. Examples:

   - I can call Jane and ask her directly if she
     loves me.

   - I can talk about my nervousness with the
     audience rather than trying to hide it.

The Genius Move has many benefits, but the one
you will usually notice first happens right in your body.
If you pay close attention to your body sensations, you
will likely notice a new feeling of more space in your
body—an expansive sense of liberation from the bondage of your effort to control. You may notice you're
breathing easier as the overall relief of acceptance comes
over you.

All you have to do is this:

*Notice a moment when you're feeling unhappy for whatever reason.*

*Ask yourself, "What am I trying to control that's actually uncontrollable?"*

*Declare it uncontrollable and let it be. Say in your mind or out loud, "I consciously let go of trying to control it, whatever it is."*

*Look for a positive action you can take right now.*

Then tune in with your natural awareness to the sensations in your body. See if you notice a new sense of ease spreading through you. It may come in like a whisper at first, but the more you devote your attention to it, the clearer the sweet feeling of liberation will be.

The feeling I'm describing is the first benefit of the Genius Move. In other words, the Genius Move feels good. It feels good the first time you do it and keeps feeling even better as you get more skilled at applying it.

The second benefit is a new way of relating to other people. The moment you let go of trying to control other people—how they feel, what they want, who they want to be—you enter into a very different relationship with them.

Relationships in which people are trying to control each other are based in fear. When I first realized this in myself, I found it difficult to admit how much I was operating out of fear. Even fear itself was hard for me to acknowledge. I grew up in an era dominated by tough-guy heroes such as John Wayne, Gary Cooper, and Humphrey Bogart. John Wayne didn't get scared or cry, and I didn't, either.

That was my story up into my twenties, but then it slowly began to dawn on me that if I wanted to have healthy relationships, particularly with women, I had to let go of my tough-guy act. My life became better the more I let go of trying to control my feelings and hide them from the world. I let myself cry again, which I hadn't done since I was in elementary school. I admitted other emotions into my mind that I must have been feeling in my body since childhood: shame, fear, anger, sexual excitement. I began to realize that each of us has a wealth of hidden emotion tucked inside. As I began to listen more to my own inner world of feeling, I also began to tune in to that world in others.

Discovering the new world of feelings revolutionized

my life. I, who had spent a lifetime assembling barriers between me and others, now suddenly had nothing to hide. I, who had spent a lifetime being largely oblivious to other people's feelings, now was willing to listen.

## The Genius Move: A Guided Meditation

To assist you in learning the Genius Move, treat yourself to the following guided meditation. It is designed specifically to help you get comfortable making the Genius Move in the "heat of action," the daily occurrences of your life.

### INSTRUCTIONS

Find a comfortable place where you won't be disturbed for ten to fifteen minutes. If possible, do this activity with a friend or partner, so that you can read the instructions to each other. If you do it on your own, pause after you read each paragraph to carry out the instruction before reading the next paragraph.

Let's begin . . .

Imagine that you are going along in your daily life, perhaps sitting at a meeting, driving a car, or talking to a loved one.

You become aware that you feel unhappiness occurring somewhere in your body and mind. Perhaps your shoulders feel tight or you are recycling unpleasant thoughts such as, "What's wrong with me?" Perhaps you are in a relationship conflict.

Suddenly you remember that when you're unhappy, you're almost always trying to control something that is beyond your power to control.

You ask yourself, "What am I trying to control that's actually not within my power to control?"

Perhaps you get an insight, perhaps you don't, but the insight is not the important part. The wondering—asking the question—is the important part of the move. Many of your biggest insights may come later that day or even at night in your dreams.

Next, whether or not you have any insight into what you're trying to control, formally declare that it is outside your control. Say in your mind or out loud, "I consciously let go of trying to control it, whatever it is." If you have an insight about the specific issue, put it in the sentence like this: "I consciously let go of trying to control whether Jane loves me or not," or, "I consciously let go of trying to control my nervousness when I speak in public."

Next you think of a positive action you can do right away, something you actually have control over.

You take the action. For example:

**I can call Jane and ask her directly if she loves me.**

**I can talk about my nervousness with the audience rather than trying to hide it.**

Finally, you enjoy the feeling of ease and clarity that comes from letting go of trying to change the unchangeable.

When you feel complete with this process, resume your normal activities.

I highly recommend repeating this guided meditation several times a week when you are first learning to master the Genius Move. Just as a gymnast mentally rehearses the backflip or a golfer pictures the trajectory of the shot, your mental run-throughs of the Genius Move can help you integrate it into your daily life.

## The Genius Move in Action Now

To end this chapter, let me share a real-life, real-time example of how I used the Genius Move about a half hour before I started writing this morning. A member of my extended family texted me last evening, asking for a loan of several thousand dollars for extra holiday expenses and to pay a tax lien. Based on her dismal record of repaying past loans (zero for five over a twenty-year period), I found myself stewing about whether to go along with the "loan" fantasy or just give her the money.

I also had a slew of other thoughts running through my mind, mostly about whether I should turn her down altogether. I didn't like the idea of perpetuating her or anybody else's dependency script. Plus, there was my growing irritation that I was being seen as her own personal ATM. Perhaps an unexpected no would shock her out of the mind-set that was creating her repetitive money dramas. Occasionally a critical thought about myself would flicker through, such as, "Maybe I'm just being stingy."

This little ping-pong match went on in my head for a few minutes while I was making my breakfast. Just before my bagel popped up out of the toaster, I remembered to apply the Genius Move. A flood of insights dawned on me in rapid order. Here's what I wrote down in my journal:

> I have absolutely no control over whether or not she ever transcends the limitations that keep her from being prosperous.
>
> I have no control over what she thinks about me or how she feels about me. It's absolutely none of my business if she feels grateful or angry or considers me her personal ATM.
>
> The only thing I have control over is whether or not I give her the money. I especially have no control over how either of us is

going to feel about it afterward. I don't know
if she'll regard me as a benign philanthropist
or a pathetic sucker, but in any case, what
she thinks is beyond my ability to control. It's
none of my business.

After making the Genius Move, I quickly came to
a decision about the money, which I'll describe in a
moment. However, the decision wasn't the remarkable
thing that happened. What really rocked me again, as
it had so many times before, was the body feeling that
came immediately after the decision.

First, here's what I decided: I offered her the money
as a gift, not a loan. In return, I asked for a verbal and
written agreement that she would not approach me about
any money-related matters for at least eighteen months. I
told her I valued our relationship and wanted to have it
be free of money topics for a while. She readily agreed.

The moment I got off the phone I felt a powerful
rush of positive energy stream up through my body.
It was an overall feeling of zest, a whole-body hum of
aliveness. I've felt it thousands of times, but every time
it happens it always feels brand new.

One of my psychotherapy mentors, the late Dr. William

Glasser, wrote a book called *Positive Addiction*. He makes the point that since addictive tendencies seem to be wired in us humans, we need to be thoughtful about choosing positive things to be addicted to. Inspired by that message, I confess to being totally and enthusiastically addicted to the rush of good feeling that comes from letting go. Not only am I hooked on it but also I go out of my way to get everybody I care about hooked. Fortunately, it's the best kind of addiction: it feels great and has only positive side effects. Even better, you can manufacture that feeling of humming aliveness yourself and nurture it until it becomes the background tone of your life.

All any of us has to do to feel that benign surge of good feeling is to perform the Genius Move:

*Notice you're feeling unhappy, regardless of the reason.*

*Wonder, "What am I trying to control that's actually impossible for me to control?"*

*Get an insight about what you've been trying to control, or if nothing comes, let your mind continue to wonder about it.*

*Acknowledge that it's outside your control, whatever it is.*

*Let it go and let it be.*

The last part of the move, the act of letting go, is what usually triggers the rush of good feeling. Since it's so important to the process, I'd like to explore it with you in more detail.

## The Art of Letting Go

The best way to learn how to let go is to start by actually letting go of something. I've used the following activity myself and have taught it to three generations of students. It teaches two different types of letting go, both of which work well. I'd like you to test them out in the laboratory of your own body to see which one feels better to you.

### HANDS-ON ACTIVITY

**STEP 1**

Use your imagination to get a sense of the first way of letting go. Picture yourself with your arm outstretched, holding a tennis ball in your hand, ball downward, with your fingers gripping the ball to keep it from dropping to the floor. In your imagination, feel how it would be to hold the ball.

Now imagine letting the tension go from your hand, loosening your grip until the ball naturally falls and bounces on the floor.

That's the first way to let go: by loosening a grip on something and letting it drop.

**STEP 2**

Get an actual ball or some other object you can safely drop. A pencil will do, or even a wadded-up ball of paper.

Stretch your arm out with the object in your hand, facing downward, so that your hand must grip it to keep it from dropping. Grip it for a long moment, perhaps ten seconds, then release your grip and let it drop to the floor.

Immediately pick it up and repeat the process: grip it and let it drop. Do that a few times to get the actual physical feeling of letting something go so that it drops out of your grip.

**A SECOND WAY OF LETTING GO**

**Step 1**

Again, use your imagination to begin. Picture yourself with an arm outstretched, but this time your palm is facing upward as you grip a ball or other small object. Feel how it would be to grip the object in your hand, palm up. Then, in your imagination, release your grip and let the object rest in the palm of your hand. You've still got the object in the palm of your hand, but now you have a different relationship with it. You are letting it be.

**STEP 2**

Place the actual ball or object in the palm of your hand, facing upward. Stretch your arm out and hold your grip on the object for ten seconds or so. Then, release your grip and let the object rest lightly in the palm of your hand. Play with how to hold the object in the most comfortable way.

Let go by dropping it or let go by letting it be—it never gets any more complicated than that. Notice the grip, release the grip, and let it drop or let it be. It's the simplest thing in the world and yet so hard for most of us to learn in real life. Fortunately, the universe in its wisdom gifts us with many opportunities to practice the art of letting go. I've been working and playing with the concept of letting go for more than half my life now, and I hope to keep learning about it until my last whisper.

# 3

# FREEING UP MIND-SPACE FOR
# GENIUS TO EMERGE

## *How to End Your Specific Type
## of Negative Thinking*

Here's another piece of wisdom it took me half a lifetime to learn:

The biggest barrier blocking our path to genius is a habit of fear-based negative thinking. Putting an end to the habit is a powerful investment in our genius. Paradoxically, our struggle with negative thinking ends only when we declare we have no control over it.

That paradox changed my life, but at first it really flummoxed my mind. It had never occurred to me that the only way to stop my negative thoughts was to let go of trying to stop them! Some of the ways I'd been trying to control my negative thoughts—by shaming myself for thinking them or trying to engage in positive thinking—actually turned out to be the glue that held them in place.

For example, when you find yourself in a stream of negative thoughts, you either continue to dwell on them or look for some way to get out of the stream. That's a key moment, because what you decide to do determines whether you'll be happy or not.

Many people make a costly mistake at that moment: they go into some form of combat with their negative thoughts. One type of combat is to criticize yourself for your negative thoughts, as I did, attempting to shame them into submission. Eventually we discover it's futile to try to get rid of negative thoughts by bombarding them with more negative thoughts. Like a dog chasing its own tail, you end up just going around in circles.

Even though it goes back half a lifetime, I can still remember the jolt of awakening to how much I was trying to get rid of my negative thoughts by aiming negative thoughts at them. I realized I'd been playing host to a circular shooting match in my head, trying to kill off my thoughts of disappointment and misery by firing off a constant rat-a-tat of shame and blame at them.

I also saw the futility of trying to counteract my negative thinking by paving over it with positive thoughts. No matter how many times I read *The Power of Positive Thinking* by Norman Vincent Peale, my negative thoughts would always come back to annoy and depress me.

Then I discovered the paradoxical miracle I'm describing: the only way to change negative thinking begins with acknowledging that you have no control over it. By this application of the Genius Move, you are able to withdraw the energy you've been expending trying to control negative thinking. Then, you can redirect that energy to those things you actually have the ability to change.

I found this concept a slippery one to get hold of at first. Let me give you an example of how it works in real life.

I've worked with many clients who have benefited greatly from AA and other twelve-step programs. One of them, a heroic fellow I'll call Jay, not only found his own sobriety but also went on to sponsor more than six hundred recovering alcoholics over many decades.

Jay told me about a life-changing moment: the first time he stood up and spoke at an AA meeting. He said, "My name's Jay, and I'm an alcoholic. And I have no idea how I'm going to stop drinking." He told me it was a moment of clarity like nothing he had ever experienced before.

"I suddenly felt lighter than air," he said, "like I'd been released from carrying a heavy burden up in my head." For the past twenty years, he'd been shaming himself for his drinking, always apologizing and promising to do better; but on that magic day he did something radically different. For twenty years, he'd been telling his concerned family and friends that he wasn't an alcoholic, that he could control his drinking. All the while, though, he had kept creating messes in his life that told a different story.

Then came the moment when he stood up in public, owned his addiction, and declared it was out of his control. This radical act of transparency and acceptance brought a new sense of lightness to him; with the support of the group, he got through his first day in twenty years without a drink. Then he went back to a meeting the next day and was able to chalk up two days in a row of sobriety. By the time I met Jay, he'd racked up more than five thousand of those days without a drink, while also helping hundreds of others find their sobriety. To me, that's a hero's journey equal to anything Odysseus turned in.

I particularly resonated with Jay's description of the lightness he felt, because it was so similar to what had happened for me. The moment I let go of trying to control all the things nobody can control, I actually felt two forms of lightness come over me. My whole inner world lit up, as if I were emerging from the shadows of my old negative thinking. I also felt the kind of lightness Jay mentioned—the sense of shedding a heavy load I'd been carrying for a long time.

When I first began to uncover the tools I'm sharing with you in this book, I was twenty-four years old and weighed three hundred pounds rather than this morning's one hundred and eighty-five. I couldn't go more than twenty minutes without a cigarette, I hated my job, and I felt trapped in an awful relationship. Within a year or so after the discovery, I dropped my addictions, shed more than a hundred pounds, got out of the toxic relationship, and embarked on a new career. To say it changed my life would be an understatement. It *gave* me my life.

I'm convinced that if I had continued the way I was going, I would have replayed my father's brief existence. He died at age thirty-two, grossly obese, a heavy smoker, and stuck in a job he didn't like. I feel sad to this day that he never got to live out his full life span and I never got to know him.

I also feel incredibly grateful that I woke up in time to change the direction of my life. Sometimes I feel regret that it took me so long to figure out something so simple, but most days I feel grateful that I figured it out at all. Whether you are twenty-four or forty-four or eighty-four when you are reading or hearing this, take comfort from knowing that it is never too late to release your old programming. Like every one of us, you just have to start wherever you are.

## Two Kinds of Thoughts

If you train your awareness on the contents of your thought stream for a while, you will discover something that may surprise you. I know it surprised me when I first caught sight of it.

Your mind only thinks two kinds of thoughts: thoughts about things you can control and thoughts about things you cannot control. The majority of the thoughts that pass through your mind are about things you cannot control.

Dwelling on thoughts about things you can't control causes a massive amount of pain and suffering in the world. The ability to think is a precious human resource, but many of us squander that gift by thinking about things that make us miserable and that we cannot change. Meanwhile, we often overlook or fail to do the simple things we could change on the spot.

There's a time and place for thinking about things you have no control over, such as when you're using the power of your imagination to create or design something new. That's a conscious use of thinking about things you have no control over. The problem begins when your unconscious mind gets hold of the thinking machinery and starts cranking out thoughts that make you unhappy.

Letting our minds continue to produce thoughts that make us unhappy is letting the tail wag the dog. If allowed to continue in that direction, our minds eventually become all tail and no dog, wagging on into eternity for no conscious purpose, making us miserable all the way.

## The Problem of Incompletion

One of the most popular ways we create unconscious mayhem in our lives is through leaving situations and communications incomplete. When I first started noticing this in my own life, I was surprised to discover how often I walked away from conversations without completing them, leaving unsaid what was really on my mind or in my heart. As I expanded my awareness of incompletion, I realized that it wasn't just conversations I left incomplete.

I started making a list of various incompletions, stretching back into childhood: people I hadn't thanked for their kindness to me, a former employer I'd borrowed $160 from and hadn't paid back, abuses I hadn't confronted, and many more. My list ultimately ran to twelve pages, single-spaced. I was a virtual master of incompletion.

Incompletion works like the snooze alarm feature on an alarm clock. When the alarm buzzes, the sleepy person gropes for the clock and punches the snooze button, making the alarm stop buzzing. A few minutes later, the noisome buzz drones into your awareness again. In college, I had to put my alarm clock on the other side of the room to keep me from irresponsible use of my snooze alarm. Otherwise I'd keep reaching over and hitting it until noon.

Here's how incompletion causes trouble for us in real life. I had a rude wake-up moment early in my career as a professor at the University of Colorado. My counseling department locked horns repeatedly with a dean who didn't like some of the nontraditional things we did in our program. For example, we always took the new students on a weekend camping retreat at the beginning of the academic year. Although I am not an enthusiastic camper (full transparency: I hate camping), I always participated, because the retreat had a valuable bonding effect on the students.

The dean hated this sort of unorthodox learning, but he couldn't stop us, because the counseling program was by far the most popular one in the entire graduate school. Anytime he threatened us, we would respond with an equally dire threat to admit fewer students. Since the budget and his overinflated salary—three times what the other professors and I made—were dependent on the large number of students in the counseling program, he would huff and puff for a few days, then quiet down.

One day I was driving home after a meeting where the dean had been on one of his rants. I had left the meeting steamed up and found myself furiously replaying the conversation over and over, each time inventing new and more devastating responses that proved how right I was and how wrong he was.

At a stoplight, I was so caught up in my mental argument that I failed to notice that the light had turned green. The motorists behind me began to serenade me with a chorus of their horns. The blaring noise startled me out of my trance and I accelerated jerkily, stalling my engine. Another round of horns honking blatted behind me before I recovered and got underway.

A half mile down the road, though, the mental argument with the dean returned at full force. There I was again, back in the dean's office in my mind, firing off all the devastatingly cutting remarks I hadn't said in the actual meeting.

I found myself wondering, "Where had the argument gone during my episode at the traffic light? And why had it come back?"

Two insights came in rapid order. First, I realized I was trying to control and change the past, which was not controllable by me or anybody else. I also realized that the argument in my mind had begun and returned for the same reason: incompletion.

Much of our negative thinking comes from leaving situations incomplete. There's an old scientific saying that nature abhors a vacuum. An incompletion is a kind of vacuum, and from personal experience I can testify that nature doesn't like it very much, either.

When we leave a situation incomplete, nature will find a way to keep reminding us of the incompletion. Nature seeks completion and will propel us to great lengths to get it.

For example, my situation with the dean is similar to something almost everyone experiences at one time or another. I left the conversation without being fully transparent about my real feelings. I left with feelings in my body that my mouth hadn't spoken.

Leaving a conversation without saying what we really need to say probably happens more often than its opposite. When we leave a conversation without fully revealing what's on our minds and in our hearts, a pressure begins to build inside us. The force of nature then propels us to seek completion.

I remember seeing a film of Yellowstone National Park's Old Faithful when I was in elementary school, marveling at how its eruptions went off predictably every hour or so. The pressure would build for an hour, then it would start sending up mini belches of steam and water, early warning signs of the eruption to come. Then *BOOM!* The water would explode a hundred feet up into the air.

In one respect, human beings are like Old Faithful;

but in another way, we are strictly Old Unfaithful. We are predictable in the sense that pressure builds in us, propelling us toward completion. Unlike Old Faithful, though, with humans you never quite know when the eruption is going to occur.

Here's a particularly vivid example of the unpredictability of completion. A client of mine, a successful entrepreneur in his midforties, told me that he was having a pleasant after-dinner conversation over a glass of wine with his wife one evening when a sudden urge to confess came over him. We'll never know if it was a sudden surge of character strength or the effects of a second glass of wine, but in the midst of the conversation he blurted out a truth that had been building inside him for a year. He said, "I've been having an affair with your best friend."

He told me he'd started to confess the affair on several other occasions, but he had been unable to get the words out of his mouth. Finally, he could no longer contain the truth and it broke through that night.

Nature is always seeking completion. A stream completes itself by joining the river; the river yearns for completion in the ocean. Completion is a powerful force. Over time, water's desire for completion can carve out a

Grand Canyon. When we resist its power, we create all manner of unhappiness for ourselves.

(For a deep dive into this subject in your own life, please take the Completions Checklist in Appendix B.)

## Completion in Relationships

Katie and I met in 1980 and have been together ever since. I'm very grateful I didn't meet her until I was in my thirties, because during my teens and twenties I made just about every relationship mistake possible. I still wince at some of those memories, such as having a secret affair or the teenage humiliation of begging my first love not to dump me.

It took me a long time to realize that many of my incompletions reached far back into childhood. In other words, I discovered that conflicts in my present-day relationships were replays of childhood dramas. For example, several years before I met Katie I was in an on-again, off-again relationship with a woman I'll call Nora. We really cared for each other, but we also really hated some things about each other. For example, she was perpetually trying to quit smoking cigarettes. I had gone through the unpleasant experience of kicking cigarettes cold turkey several years before I met her, and like many former addicts, I had become militantly judgmental on the subject.

When Nora would fall off the wagon and greet me with cigarette breath, I would freak out or storm out or lash out with verbal criticism. At the time, my mother was dying of emphysema caused by fifty years of heavy smoking. Every whiff of Nora's Marlboro breath triggered anger and sadness about the way my mother's addictions had consumed so much of her life.

Nora's freak-out pattern involved my travel. My first book came out just after we met and became a surprise bestseller in the field of education. It led to speaking engagements and invitations to present seminars all over the country. At the time, I was an assistant professor at the University of Colorado, earning thirteen thousand dollars a year. Within a few months after the book's publication, I found myself often making more in a month than I did all year in my academic job. I was still carrying a burdensome chunk of student loan debt from my Stanford years, so I very much appreciated this unexpected, good turn in my fortunes.

My newfound abundance and fame were great for me; I was flying all over the country, having the time of my life. Nora, not so much. Her father was a traveling salesman whose travels often involved cheating on Nora's mother. Because he was on the road two weeks out of every month, her father's affairs were a constant source of uproar in the family. Finally, after years of apologies and promises to do better, he gave Nora's mother a beating and never came back.

It was a perfect setup for conflict between Nora and me: two interlocking patterns that reached back into the most painful corners of our childhoods. We were each using our relationship to complete issues that were decades old. The real problem, though, was that neither of us had the slightest clue that we were being run by those ancient patterns. We just mindlessly repeated the same arguments month after month. The more Nora criticized me for being away so much, the more I wanted to get away. The more I criticized her for smoking, the more often she came back reeking of cigarettes.

One weekend while speaking at a conference, I had a steamy backstage kiss with a lovely woman who was also presenting a seminar at the conference. That evening after we finished up our teaching chores, we indulged in even steamier activities that didn't end until room service breakfast the next morning. We parted with a friendly hug, knowing it was unlikely we would ever connect again in that particular way. It was an altogether delightful interlude, except for one problem: it left me with a big incompletion.

The month before, in one of my attempts to quiet Nora's traveling salesman fears, I had assured her I would not engage in any romantic activities while I was on the road. I hadn't liked making the agreement with her; something in me knew it wouldn't solve the problem. I did it anyway, and now I was carrying the burden of a secret and a broken promise.

This incompletion set up a rattle that finally ended the relationship. I hung on to the secret for a week, then a month. During that time, I noticed that my mind was jammed with thoughts devoted to explaining and justifying my behavior. For example, I'd catch myself saying in my mind, "I don't need to tell Nora about this, because she probably keeps a lot of secrets from me," and, "I don't need to tell Nora because it would be too upsetting for her." I also noticed a sharp escalation in the number of my critical thoughts about Nora.

Does any of this sound familiar to you? Before I tell you more of the story, take a moment to explore explaining and justifying in an experiential fashion.

## HANDS-ON ACTIVITY

Pause to reflect on this question from your own experience: Is your negative thinking flavored with explaining and justifying? In other words, do you find yourself explaining things to people in your mind and justifying why you did or didn't do certain things? If so, note this particular flavor of negative thinking and acknowledge it consciously by writing the following commitment out in longhand:

*I commit to learning how I make myself unhappy by explaining and justifying.*

As always when you are doing Hands-On Activities in this book, notice your breathing and body sensations as you make the commitment. Notice if making the commitment stirs up fear, sadness, or other emotions.

The goal of this activity is to focus your attention on the relationship between unhappiness and the mental activities of explaining and justifying. The goal is not to get rid of explaining and justifying, because they both have their healthy, positive uses. For example, if you are called on in math class to explain the quadratic equation, use every bit of your skill at explanation. The same goes for justifying. If your boss asks you to justify your budget requests for the year, use all your skills of justification to make your points. There's a downside, however, to mental skills such as explaining and justifying. They get us in trouble when we use them in ways that perpetuate unhappiness in our lives.

That's why I want you to put a bright spotlight on the explaining and justifying that goes on in your mind. You will probably notice, as I did, that most of the time I was explaining or justifying something in my mind, I was also feeling unhappy. It took me quite a while to figure out the relationship between the two.

I discovered that every time I found myself explaining and justifying something, I could trace that "something" back to an incompletion. For example, I could have called Nora the morning after my wayward tryst and said, "Nora, I broke my agreement not to have romantic adventures on my travels." If she were interested in the details, as I suspect she would have been, I could have given them to her.

But I didn't do any of that. Instead I stewed in the incompletion as one month turned into two, meanwhile feeling more and more unsettled inside every day. Finally, though, the truth broke through at an odd moment.

I was riding my bicycle to my office one warm day when suddenly I felt a rush of sadness and started sobbing uncontrollably. The surge of feeling seemed to come out of nowhere with an unexpected intensity. One moment I was puffing along at a rapid clip on the bike path, the next moment I was sobbing so hard it was all I could do to wobble to a stop.

It didn't take a lot of wondering to understand what the tears were about. Images of hiding the truth and lying to Nora were streaming through my mind. It felt like the cells of my body were screaming at me, "You can't keep going like this."

I saw clearly what I needed to do. When my tears subsided, I jumped back on my bike and went off in search of a phone booth.

Note to younger readers: There was actually a time when you couldn't walk around with a phone in your hand! In those days, we phoned from our homes on large, clunky devices attached to the wall. If we were away from home and needed to make a call, we had to go in search of a public phone. These were often housed in smelly little huts, along with a directory missing half its pages and a lot of intriguing inscriptions scribbled on the interior walls. You also had to have a pocketful of dimes and quarters to feed the phone.

I located a phone booth and used up my dimes tracking Nora down. I caught her just leaving work and arranged to meet her at her apartment. I pedaled over in a throat-clutching state of anxiety all the way. As soon as I got face-to-face with Nora, I opened my mouth and unburdened myself.

It only took me ten seconds or so to tell her what I'd done, but Nora took at least ten torturous minutes expressing her strong feelings on the matter. Although I winced at Nora's vigorous assault on my character, I also noticed something surprising going on in my body, an unexpected positive feeling. It was an exhilarating sense of liberation flowing through me. For the first time in weeks I felt like I could take a deep breath. I was free from the bondage of concealment.

As Nora's tirade wound down, I had the hopeful thought that she might thank me for my honesty and wrap me in a forgiving hug. It didn't quite work out that way. Nora pointed to the door and told me to get the hell out.

I saddled up and pedaled home, contemplating the lessons life had just served up to me:

**Life lesson #1:** *When I hide the truth, I hurt. Telling the truth makes me feel better.*

**Life lesson #2:** *People don't always jump for joy and thank me when I reveal the truth to them.*

I realized I'd been running a con on myself since childhood. The lie I'd been telling myself went like this: "I hide the truth from people because they'll feel bad if I tell them. I want them to feel good, so it's okay to lie to them. If I lie to people, it's for their own good."

The real reason was not so flattering: "I hide the truth from people because I don't want to have to deal with their reactions. I don't want to deal with their anger or hurt or punishment or whatever other feelings they might have."

Later that day I wrote in my journal, "I vow from here on out to reveal instead of conceal. I have no control over how people are going to react to the truth. The only thing I can control is whether or not I speak honestly. It's ultimately not my business to manage anybody else's emotions."

At some point in our evolution, all of us need to answer a fundamental question: "Do I prefer to have people tell me the truth, or do I want them to lie to me so my feelings don't get hurt?"

I've asked that question to audiences all over the world, and whether they're in Beijing or Brooklyn, they always tell me the same thing: "I want to hear the unvarnished truth. I don't want anybody to lie to me to protect my feelings."

When I turn the question around, though, a sudden silence often descends on the room. I ask them, "Do you speak the truth scrupulously to people you care about, or do you sometimes lie to them to spare their feelings?" Overwhelmingly, no matter if the audience is speaking English, Spanish, or Chinese, they admit they habitually conceal the truth so as not to push the emotional buttons of others.

The conclusion: we don't want to be lied to ourselves, but we assume other people want us to lie to them.

I want to live a different kind of life than that. I want a life based on honest communication and generous listening. I bet that's what you want, too. I also want us to create a different kind of world from the one we live in today, where the falsehoods come at us so fast it's hard to keep up with them all.

That new world gets created one choice at a time. It gets created when you choose to reveal rather than conceal, when you choose to listen mindfully rather than indulge in old assumptions.

Take a moment right now to stake your place in that new world.

**HANDS-ON ACTIVITY**

Get paper and a writing instrument.

Consider this commitment:

I commit to speaking honestly and listening mindfully.

Listening mindfully means to listen without interrupting or criticizing what the other person is saying. Of course, making the commitment won't guarantee that you will always speak honestly and listen mindfully, but you have to start somewhere. The best place to start is with a commitment. A commitment is a stand you take. It's a declaration.

If you would like to take such a stand, write the following sentence out three times:

*I commit to speaking honestly and listening mindfully.*

As always when you do the Hands-On Activities, notice your breathing and other body signals that occur while you're writing out the commitment.

## Relationships Are the Ultimate Test

Honesty with ourselves is essential, but it is in the area of relationships where our commitment to honest speaking and mindful listening gets tested most rigorously.

In my own case, committing to honesty not only made my public-speaking life very simple but it also revolutionized my personal life. I'm convinced that it led me on a direct line to a moment of destiny in 1980, when I showed up to give a talk and seminar in Menlo Park, California.

In the audience that day was a professional in her early thirties named Kathlyn, who would eventually be known to millions by her nickname of Katie. We've described our amazing first meeting in detail in other books, but, briefly, the key part of the conversation went something like this.

Me: I'm very attracted to you. I'd like to ask you out for coffee, but first I need to let you know I have only recently figured out what I really want. I'm only interested in relationships where both people tell the truth, take responsibility for what's going on with them instead of blaming, and are passionately committed to their creative development. On those terms, would you like to have coffee with me?

There was a ten-second pause while she contemplated this unusual pickup line. Then . . .

Katie: How about lunch?

By the time I met Katie, I had grown militant about what I wanted in a relationship. The three wants I presented to Katie—honesty, responsibility, and creative commitment—all had come from doing the exact opposite in other relationships. Essentially, they represented the most painful learning experiences of my life. Sometimes I created misery in my love life by lying (or failing to notice that the other person was lying to me). Other times I made myself miserable by blaming the other person rather than owning responsibility for whatever was going on.

A third misery-making pattern of mine was to get into relationships with people who were not as passionately committed to their own creative path as I was to mine. Writing is my creative passion; in its pursuit, I disappear into a room by myself for several hours almost every day. Somehow I'd managed to attract several women in a row who criticized me for my daily disappearances. I tried to deal with the issue by arranging my creative hours around their schedules, but it never seemed to alter the patterns of criticism.

Then one day truth penetrated the fog. I realized I was the actual source of the criticism, not them. I took responsibility for the pattern rather than blaming anyone else. I asked myself the question, "What is it in me that keeps attracting the same experience over and over with different women?"

I saw immediately how I'd been gestated and born

into criticism—as I've written in *The Big Leap* and elsewhere, my appearance in the world came at a most inconvenient time for several parties.

Then I was reared by my mother and grandmother, both of whom were remarkably creative women who never got to fulfill their potentials. They both felt oppressed by having to spend all their time taking care of other people, and they voiced those frustrations in more or less noisy ways on a regular basis. Now here I was, doing my own version of the same thing! It was enlightening but also horrifying to see how unconsciously I was living out a family tradition of thwarted creativity.

I added another life lesson to my growing stack: we always attract unconsciously the very things we complain about.

## Summarizing

I want you to take away several big learnings from this chapter.

First, I want you to become aware of how much unhappiness you create through entertaining negative thoughts about four main things: the past, the future, other people, and yourself.

Second, I want you know that you cannot rid yourself of negative thoughts by aiming more negative thoughts at them. You can only retire your negative thoughts by acknowledging that you have no control over them. The moment you quit fighting your thoughts, they will quit bothering you.

Finally, I want you to understand in your mind and body how the act of accepting and loving your negative thoughts, just as they are, dissolves and disappears them. This openhearted act—acknowledging your negative thoughts with acceptance rather than censure—releases your attachment to them. Your acceptance, an act of generosity on your part, opens up a new world of possibility in which your generosity can be richly rewarded.

### HANDS-ON ACTIVITY

I'd like you to finish this section with an activity that will help you lock in the key learnings from this chapter.

### INSTRUCTIONS

Get paper and a writing instrument. In your own handwriting, write out each of the following statements, paying attention to your breathing as you do so:

*I formally declare that I cannot control
my negative thoughts, and I commit to letting go
of trying to control them.*

*I commit to letting go of trying to change the past.*

*I commit to letting go of worrying about the future.*

*I commit to letting go of trying to
control other people.*

*I commit to channeling my precious energy into
positive actions I can take now.*

There are two spectacular payoffs for clearing negative thoughts out of your mind. First, your inner world becomes much more serene as the unpleasant chatter of negative thinking fades out of your experience. Second, this open space invites a new and deeper relationship with your own source of true creativity.

How to maximize this relationship is the subject of our next exploration.

# 4

# HOW TO WOO YOUR TRUE CREATIVITY

Here's a bottom-line truth I've learned, both from my own experience and from working with clients: you will never be genuinely happy unless you dedicate your body, mind, and soul to a lifelong courtship of your true creativity.

Turn that sentence into a positive prescription and it goes like this: you will feel happiest when you are fully engaged with your true creativity.

I use the word "courtship" because your true creativity needs to be wooed on a daily basis. When you are wooing a beloved, you go to extraordinary lengths to cultivate the relationship. You make space and time to be together, you speak to your beloved with kindness and respect, you celebrate her or his very existence. Your creativity needs to be wooed just like that.

## The Art of the Woo

Think of your creativity in the same way you think of a beloved partner. Katie and I started working together within a few months of falling in love. Since then we've done hundreds of seminars together, been on *Oprah* together, and written a dozen books together. Even with all this time together, I feel like I learn new things about her all the time. I fall in love with her all over again on a daily basis.

That's how I feel about my creativity, too. I've learned that my true creativity and the infinite depths of my beloved are essentially the same thing. What makes a relationship thrive is also what makes your creativity thrive.

## Creativity Thrives in Time and Space

When you are wooing a beloved, you make plenty of time for him or her. You create space so you can be together free of distraction. You do this out of the honor and respect you feel for your beloved.

I want you to feel that way about your creativity, too. Your most valuable asset is hidden in plain sight, in the innate genius that is yours to cultivate. If you want to bring it forth on an ongoing basis to nurture your whole life, you need to make space for your creativity and be rigorous about dedicating time to it.

## Making Space for Your Creativity

First, the most important step is to make a safe and welcoming inner space for your creativity. If you don't have a comfortable home for your creativity inside you, no fancy computer or elegantly appointed office can make up for the lack. Just as no mansion can make up for the lack of intimacy in a marriage, it's always what goes on inside that makes the difference.

Focus in for a moment on your overall relationship with your creativity. Begin by asking a few clarifying questions.

Ask yourself, "How much do I appreciate my creativity?"

When divorcing couples are asked why they left, one of the main answers they give is, "I didn't feel appreciated." If your creativity were a love partner, do you think it would feel appreciated?

Explore with me for a moment two main meanings of appreciation. Most often when we think of appreciating something, we mean that we are grateful for it. We say to a beloved, "I appreciate how kind you were to me when I was sick last week," or, "I appreciate your beauty." Appreciation is an expression of gratitude.

That's one important part of appreciation. But there's a second meaning that plays a key role in your relationship with your creativity.

When you appreciate something, perhaps a work of art, you tune in to it sensitively. It pleases you to see it, and you go out of your way to spend your valuable time with it.

For example, Katie and I go to New York on business every now and then, but when we're there we always do two things in our spare time. The first is a visit to the Met to see a Rembrandt self-portrait that has always moved me deeply. In fact, I burst into tears the first time I saw it half a lifetime ago, and I have made a point of visiting it many times since then. I've spent so many hours with the painting that I feel like I know Rembrandt.

The first thing I see when I appreciate the painting is how ruthlessly Rembrandt looks at his aging process. It is not a flattering portrait at all; if he had painted a client's portrait so realistically, he probably wouldn't have gotten paid. It's a man seeing himself as he is.

The second thing that leaves me in awe about the painting is the amount of emotion that looks back at us across the centuries. I see grief, resignation, and stolid acceptance showing through his eyes and the set of his expression, along with a world-weariness that lets us know he is aware of his coming infirmities.

Our second stop in New York is to visit another old friend, this one at the Museum of Modern Art: *The*

*Starry Night* by Vincent van Gogh. I also cried the first time I saw that painting. It's the only one besides the Rembrandt that has ever had that effect on me. Van Gogh painted it the year between cutting off his ear and taking his own life. In addition to its raw power and shimmering beauty, the painting to me shows a mind spinning out of control yet still maintaining the artistic commitment to turning it into art. Just as Rembrandt turned his unflinching gaze on the pouches and droops of his face, Vincent studied his own inner ferment and brought it to life in the night sky.

I appreciate both of these paintings. I appreciate them in the sense that I'm grateful for them. I also appreciate them in the sense that I tune in to them as sensitively as I can. I notice their subtleties; I communicate with them. It's one of the ways I woo my creativity.

For me, creativity thrives in an atmosphere of lavish appreciation. The more I appreciate my creativity, the more creative I get. With both types of appreciation in mind—gratitude and sensitive awareness—ask yourself, "How much do I appreciate my creativity?"

"Am I grateful for it?"

"Do I tune in to it sensitively?"

"Do I visit it every chance I get?"

Take a moment now for a deeper look at this crucial subject.

### HANDS-ON ACTIVITY

Even if you already appreciate your creativity lavishly, devote a few moments in real time right now to appreciating it a bit more.

In the quiet of your mind, with eyes closed if you wish, float the following sentence:

I'm grateful for my creativity.

Say the sentence in your mind, then pause for two easy breaths before repeating the sentence again. Continue the process for a minute or two, silently repeating the sentence and taking two easy breaths between repetitions.

When you finish, note what went on in your mind during the gaps between repetitions. Specifically, be on the lookout for cross talk after you say your sentence. Cross talk is when your mind argues with itself. As soon as you say, "I'm grateful for my creativity," another voice chimes in with, "No, you're not," or, "I don't think I'm creative." Cross talk is your mind arguing for its own limitations.

Notice if you blame or shame yourself for having cross

talk or any other reactions to the sentence. Simply notice all the reactions that come through. The goal is to increase your awareness of negative thoughts, not to censure them. Your negative thoughts will cease to bother you when you stop trying to get rid of them. Until then, do your best to give yourself loving compassion for anything that comes into your mind.

## To Woo Is to Wonder

The essence of true creativity is genuine wonder. Wonder is when your mind is roaming freely, unshackled from criticism, with total permission to explore as it pleases.

Wonder is the mind at play. By improving your skills at wondering, you can eventually turn your mind into a spacious playground. Wonder starts to play most productively the moment you dedicate yourself to learning about something you passionately want to know. A benign tension comes over you when you are focused on figuring out something really important. This kind of tension is a pleasant body hum, like the resonating waves of good feeling after a wake-up stretch. As a creative person, I've learned to savor it and woo it extravagantly.

## HANDS-ON ACTIVITY

### STEP 1

Get paper and a writing instrument, then write out in long-hand the following question:

*What do I most passionately want to learn?*

Write it out four times, pausing for two easy breaths between repetitions.

### STEP 2

Ask the same question silently in your mind, pausing for two easy breaths between repetitions. Simply repeat the question, then rest your mind for two easy breaths before repeating the question again. Don't make any effort to answer the question, although it's fine if answers spontaneously come. Just repeat the question four times, allowing two easy breaths of open space between repetitions.

### STEP 3

Do the same process, this time asking the question aloud. Repeat the question out loud four times, taking a fifteen-second pause between repetitions. Note the sound of your voice each time you speak the question. With each repetition, fine-tune the sound vibrations of your voice so that it feels most pleasing to you.

## Wonder-Questions

There's a specific type of question that propels the wonder machinery of your mind into action. I call them *wonder-questions,* and I consider them one of the great treasures of the mind. Wonder-questions are a largely untapped resource that facilitate living in your genius.

A classic example of a wonder-question is the one I asked you to write on your paper: What do I most passionately want to learn?

Consider that question for a moment and explore with me the qualities that make it a powerful tool.

A wonder-question has no right answer to it. It might inspire a dozen right answers, each one a path worth exploring.

A wonder-question takes you into infinity. There is no limit to the question of what you most passionately want to learn. There is something you passionately want to learn right now, and there may be thousands more on your earthly journey.

A wonder-question is like launching a kite into the air to play in the wind. To have the most fun, you have to let the kite be free to dance with the to-and-fro of the wind currents.

In my early years, I thought there was a right answer

for every question. As I matured, I realized that most of life's biggest questions don't have right answers at all. I found ultimately that life gets really interesting only when I wonder about everything, especially the stuff I thought I knew. One of our employees has a bumper sticker with an insightful observation on it: IF YOU'RE NOT IN A CONSTANT STATE OF AWE, YOU'RE NOT PAYING ATTEN- TION. My sentiments, exactly.

## HANDS-ON ACTIVITY

With paper and a writing instrument at hand, write the following word out in longhand:

*"Hmmm, . . . "*

It's the sound you make when you are genuinely wondering about something you really want to know. For example, "Hmmm, what would I love to have for dinner tonight?" Note that a genuine "hmmm" never has any criticism in it.

Now, sound the word out several times until it sounds pleasant to you: "Hmmm, hmmm, hmmm." I want you to get the feel of a genuine wonder-hum in your voice box.

Now, with a fresh feeling of wonder in your throat, write out three of your most essential wonder-questions. What are three things you most need to know right now in your life, the questions that would change your life most profoundly if you could figure them out? When you write them out, start each wonder-question with "Hmmm."

Examples:

*Hmmm, how can I get the love I want and need?*

*Hmmm, what can I do every day to make my marriage richer?*

*Hmmm, how can I generate plenty of money by doing what I most love to do?*

Begin by reflecting on and writing out your most important wonder-question first:

*Hmmm, _____?*

Then proceed to your second and third most important wonder-questions:

*Hmmm, _____?*

*Hmmm, _____?*

Feel free to make changes in your list in the hours and days after you do this activity. People often reshuffle their questions and come up with new ones many times until they home in on what's most important to them.

The home of your inner creative space comes naturally furnished with wonder. When you genuinely wonder, inquiring with passion and innocence into something your mind and heart really wants to know, you create a greater sense of spacious openness in your mind. Wonder opens space, which is a creative person's true home. When you live in your genius, you dwell in that spacious zone. You are home wherever you are. That said, you may want to build a physical home for your creativity, a special place touched by your own sense of aesthetics.

## Creating a Physical Home for Your Creativity

Let me make my bias clear at the beginning of our discussion: creativity itself is the highest priority—not where you practice it. While it's nice to have a comfortable office or studio to express your creativity in, it's not the essential thing.

This issue is keenly in my awareness at the time I'm writing this book, just after my area of Southern California was devastated by fires and mudslides. The firefighters beat back the blazes a couple of miles short of my own house, but three of my most creative friends—a filmmaker, an actor, and a sculptor—all lost their homes and studios. One day they were working in their chosen creative environments; the next day it was all smoking rubble.

Seeing this calamity up close reminded me to reaffirm once again that I want my creativity accessible wherever I put my body, not pegged to any particular place. I've found that I'm happiest when I don't attach my creativity to any particular room, house, or other material thing. In fact, I wrote one of my books mostly in cramped airplane seats, and most of another one I wrote amid the clatter and racket of commuter trains.

Here's a cautionary tale to illustrate the point.

I wrote *Learning to Love Yourself* in the summer of 1980, the same year I met Katie. I was living in a tiny, rented room at the time and didn't have access to a typewriter, so I wrote the whole book on legal pads with BIC pens, working on a desk I fashioned out of stacking an old wooden door on some concrete blocks. In spite of the humble circumstances of its birth, the book is still selling briskly many decades later.

Contrast that with a conversation I had at a party the same summer that I was scribbling away every day with my twenty-nine-cent BIC pens. I was chatting with several people, one of whom was a well-known psychotherapist I'll call Dr. Willis. In the course of the conversation I told them a little bit about the book I was working on. Dr. Willis sighed and said she envied me for having time to write a book, because she had been wanting to write a book for many years. One of the people in the conversation, another therapist, asked her why she hadn't started it yet. (One advantage of being a therapist is that you can ask nosy questions at parties and nobody seems to mind.)

She shook her head and said it wasn't the right time yet. She said her husband and she were building their dream house, which was going to have her own writing studio out back. She said she was going to start her book as soon as they got settled in the house.

You can probably guess what happened. A year or so later I heard that she and her husband had gotten into repeated conflicts over construction costs and other details of the dream house. They ultimately split up before they ever got to move in. The book never got written, either.

So we all need to think carefully before we put any conditions on our creativity, such as needing a particular time or place to make it happen. One of my writer heroes, William Faulkner, did some of his finest writing in the back room of a post office where he was supposed to be sorting mail. (Faulkner also wrote one of the greatest letters of resignation ever, handing in this succinct gem when he finally chucked his post office job: "As long as I live under the capitalistic system, I expect to have my life influenced by the demands of moneyed people. But I will be damned if I propose to be at the beck and call of every itinerant scoundrel who has two cents to invest in a postage stamp. This, sir, is my resignation.")

Christy Brown, his body twisted since birth by cerebral palsy, used his toes to type his bestseller, *My Left Foot*, which inspired the Daniel Day-Lewis movie of the same name. Viktor E. Frankl hid scribbled pages of his classic, *Man's Search for Meaning*, in the lining of the coat he wore while imprisoned in a concentration camp during the Second World War. Mozart wrote his *Requiem* bundled up in overcoats in an unheated room.

These days I do my writing in a comfortable study decorated with art we've collected over five decades, festively bedecked with flowers Katie gets from the farmers' market on Sundays. It's full of magical surprises that visitors exclaim over, such as a Charles Bragg painting, a bamboo blowgun from Borneo, a collection of Incan whistling bottles, and my collection of musical instruments—including a trombone, a shakuhachi flute, a bass ukulele, and a guitar—plus a thousand or so books I treasure.

When the Southern California fires of late 2017 came surging over the hills toward our town, Katie and I had to face the very real possibility that our magical creative space might go up in smoke. We were just leaving Singapore at the end of a ten-day Asian trip, when our house sitter called to say the area was being evacuated. We spent a seemingly eternal fourteen hours in the air, not knowing whether our beloved home would still be in existence when we landed. Somewhere out over the Pacific, though, we got very clear about what was important and what was not.

We knew that our two feline family members, Greta and Ali, were safe with our cat sitter at a beach house. We raised a glass of champagne to toast the glorious home we'd lived in for the greatest fifteen years of our lives. We saluted the art we'd collected, the jewelry Katie loved, and all the other treasures within its walls. We said a prayer for its well-being, filed it under "Things We Absolutely Cannot Control," then snuggled down under a blanket and took a nap. Thanks to good fortune and heroic firefighters, our home survived so that I'm able to write today in the magical space of my office.

Your circumstances will likely change many times

during your life, so your first commitment, like mine, must be to creativity itself. With that foundation, I encourage you to create whatever physical space pleases you. Make it humble or make it grand, furnish it according to your whims, spiritual inclinations, and artistic sensibilities. I want you to be happy wherever you are, but if you can construct a happy place for your creativity in the physical world, good on you.

Fortunately, I'm blessed with a wife who has amazing artistic sensibilities. During the years we've lived in this house, Katie has turned my home office into a work of art. If it weren't for her, I'd probably be writing in some version of the bare room I wrote *Learning to Love Yourself* in.

If you're not aesthetically inclined, engage a friend or professional in fine-tuning a creative space to your own specifications. For example, I like a neat environment, but I'm also inclined to leave a lot of messes around. Over the course of a week my desk slowly disappears under a mound of paper. I leave books scattered around, and I have been known to overlook the imminent death of a houseplant.

Fortunately, many years ago I took a clear-eyed look at my woeful lack of organizing skill and decided to hand it off to someone who was good at it. I hired an organizing genius named Allassandra who comes in from time to time to restore order. Best of all, she seems to love organizing things. She goes about it with a smile on her face, which is always a good thing to have around the office. If you're not skilled at organizing, you can probably find an Allassandra nearby who will take delight in tidying up your life.

## Making Time for Your Creativity

I've heard many people say they would express more of their creativity if they had more time. I grew up hearing this sentiment expressed on a regular basis by members of my own family. My mother was a newspaper columnist who wanted to write novels, my aunt next door was an elementary school teacher who wanted to be a writer-illustrator, and her husband was a sign painter who wanted to be an artist. Nobody ever had the time to do what they really wanted to do. Or so they said.

As I got into my cynical teenage years, I began to wonder if time was really the problem. The very same people who complained they didn't have time to write or paint somehow found the time to polish off a bottle of vodka and a pack of Camels in the evening. As I ventured more out into the world, I discovered it was full of people who coped with the pain of creative stagnation by numbing it out with addictions. When I had my wake-up moment at age twenty-four, I realized to my horror that I'd become one of those people who were stagnating creatively and covering it with addictions. I was unconsciously re-creating the same family pattern I'd criticized my elders for as a teenager.

Now, half a century away from that original awakening, I feel a great deal of compassion for all of us who are unable for whatever reason to express our creativity. Wherever we are, at whatever age, we are all faced with the same question: How committed am I to the full expression of my creativity? The question is an urgent one, because, whether you're twenty-one or eighty-one years of age, we are all propelled by a deep urge to bring our unique gifts to the world.

## The Wow of Creativity

Creativity is one of the best shows nature puts on. Everything we are now—our bodies, our brains, our quadrillion cells—got here through infinite displays of creativity by a nature that is always inventing anew.

Our human creativity is certainly a marvel, but

the feats of creativity throughout all of nature fill the mind with awe. For example, there was that long span, more than a hundred million years, when nature was experimenting with dinosaurs. We humans and our ancestors have only been around a couple of million years; we are virtual cosmic pikers compared with the dinosaurs. We don't know yet how our experiment is going to turn out, especially since, unlike those dinosaurs, we big-brained humans have managed to invent the means of our own destruction. In only a couple of million years of our human experiment—a mere blink of the eye in cosmic time—we already have enough nuclear bombs stashed in places such as North Dakota and Kazakhstan to wipe out everything but the cockroaches.

If our species disappears, though, nature will likely keep creating new forms. Just as a creative urge runs through all of nature, that spark of creativity runs through us, too. To honor it is to honor nature itself.

One way to honor your creativity is to support it in yourself. However, we live in a world of relationships with other people. For that reason, we need to examine closely how those relationships support or sabotage our creativity.

## Building Relationships That Support Your Creativity

A lot us live in relationships that stifle our creativity. I know. I used to be in one of them. Even worse, when I finally extricated myself from that painful relationship, I jumped right into another one just like it. I'll tell you the story in a moment, but first, here's the big idea I want to get across.

To fully bring forth your genius, you need to create relationships around you with people who honor and support your creativity. In my experience, it often takes more than a few sweaty conversations to make that happen. Much of the work is learning to say no to people and things that don't support your commitment to creativity. I did not find that an easy thing to do. It's essential work, though, if you want to live in your Genius Zone.

## Riffing Your Rolodex

If you were born in the digital age and don't know what a Rolodex is, it's like the contacts on your phone. The term "RIF" comes from a military command— "reduction in force." During peacetime, militaries must "riff" their troops and officer corps to trim down the budget. Whatever we call it, it's the process of eliminating from your life everyone who doesn't support your creativity.

To do that, you have to sort carefully through the people with whom you spend your time and energy. Think of each key person in your life with this question in mind: Does this person value my creativity and support it demonstrably?

When I first started my own RIF, I found it more of a challenge than I expected. The first part wasn't hard—it was easy to see which people did and which people didn't value and support my creativity. The hard part was consciously choosing to withdraw time and energy from those people.

That decision led to some intense conversations with people close to me, because some of the main ones who didn't value and support my creativity were living under my own roof. It took a lot of those stressful conversations with a lot of people to get the quality of genius connection I've enjoyed with my friends and family for the last few decades, but every one of them was worth it.

All those conversations led me to an unexpected conclusion: the issue never has anything to do with other people. It was about my not being fully committed to my own creativity. The fact that I had surrounded myself with people who didn't appreciate and encourage my creativity brought me to a humbling discovery. I had an unconscious commitment to keeping my creative potential repressed. It wasn't them—it was me.

That was the big breakthrough for me. I stopped blaming anybody else and started taking personal responsibility for creating my own situation. Doing that unleashed a power in me I didn't know I had. I didn't realize it at the time, but I had accidentally stumbled on one of life's biggest secrets: letting go of blame frees up mind-space and invites forth your natural creativity to fill the void.

I had my baggage to deal with, having grown up around people tormented by their unfulfilled creativity. Given my programming, it's not surprising that I would begin my journey in exactly the same footsteps.

Wherever your footsteps have brought you, take the bold next step of finding out how you may be bargaining away your creative power. A quick Hands-On Activity will help you find out.

## HANDS-ON ACTIVITY

Get paper and a writing instrument. With instrument in hand, write out the following sentence at least three times, filling in the blank with something different each time. Permit yourself to be candid and unenlightened in your responses to this prompt:

*I would express my creativity fully if*

_____.

*I would express my creativity fully if*

_____.

*I would express my creativity fully if*

_____.

(For example, "I would express my creativity fully if I didn't have to take care of three kids, a spouse, a dog, and a house"; "I would express my creativity fully if I had a better computer"; or "I would express my creativity fully if I weren't shy.")

The goal is to clear out of your head and put onto paper any limitations that you believe are keeping you from expressing your full creativity.

After you've generated at least three sentences, apply the antidote by reaffirming your commitment to your true creativity right this moment. Write out the following sentence three times, pausing for two easy breaths between repetitions. Write this in big, bold letters, as if you're staking a bold claim on the future:

*I commit to expressing my true creativity and enjoying every moment.*

*I commit to expressing my true creativity and enjoying every moment.*

*I commit to expressing my true creativity and enjoying every moment.*

## It's Okay to Be a Happy Genius

You'll notice that I slipped a new concept into your last three sentences—enjoying your genius. I think it's important to cultivate consciously our capacity for joy. As we grow up, choruses of voices tell us to beware of feeling too good. I got a lot of that counsel growing up, to the point of thinking that the purpose of life was to see how much pain I could endure without flinching.

Thankfully, I came to my senses. I realized that at its best, life is about having a great time while assisting others in having a great time, too. We've had plenty of miserable geniuses who have made others around them miserable. Now our world needs a new type of genius. We need people to open up to the creative genius that lies within them and generate good times around them while they do it. We need people who live in their Genius Zone and inspire others to live in theirs.

You and I are living in an era of unprecedented danger, a time when world leaders hurl Twitter taunts at each other about the size of their warheads. At the same time, all you have to do is look around at our tiny phones, our electric cars, and other miracles of technology, and you can see we are also living in a time of limitless creative opportunity. The creative tension between those two polar-opposite states is, I believe, calling forth epic new dimensions of creativity from us.

In other words, I believe that the conditions of the world are calling us to live in our genius. Whoever we are and wherever we live, you and I are being called on to bring forth the very essence of what we have to contribute. The rewards are immense, magnificent, and often immediate, but it gets even better: as you contact your unique genius and bring it forth to the world, you also discover that the gifts flow both ways. When you bring forth your own innate genius, your gift to the world is also a gift to yourself.

Our last chapter explores how to organize your creative life so that you maximize the flow of your gift-giving genius.

# 5

## THREE BOXES AND A SPIRAL

### *A New Way to Organize Your Life in the Genius Zone*

I n this chapter I want to show you a new way to organize your life so that you woo and bring forth your genius. In our seminars, we use a graphic that participants find useful in simplifying the process. Please take a look at the graphic on the next page, then I'll explain how to use it.

### Learning to Use the Graphic

Working from the bottom of the graphic upward, focus your attention on the Incompetence Box.

Many people waste a great deal of their creative time

and energy doing things they are not good at. In your Incompetence Box, make a list of at least three things you persist in doing that you aren't any good at. (Taxes,

**My Genius Spiral**

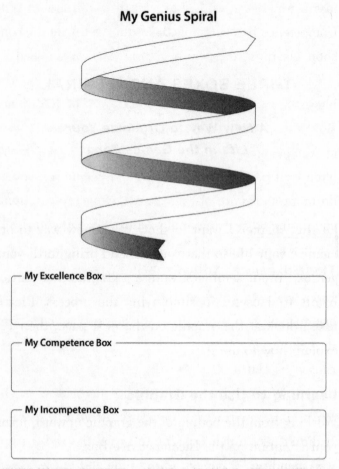

- My Excellence Box

- My Competence Box

- My Incompetence Box

organizing, computers, and plumbing are popular examples.)

Many others squander their creative energy doing things they are good at but that someone else could do just as well or better. List at least three of these in your Competence Box (examples: standing in line at the copy shop, cleaning your house, getting your car serviced).

Getting stuck in your Excellence Box is by far the biggest burner of genius energy. List in your Excellence Box at least three things you do that you're really good at. You get good feedback on how you do them, you are often well paid for doing them, and people ask you to do more and more of them (e.g., giving presentations, composing advertising jingles, editing documentaries).

## The Boxes Sap Your Creative Energy

From working with creative people in just about every major line of work, from medicine to management to metaphysics, I have seen up close the unhappiness caused by getting stuck in the three boxes. I've felt it myself. When I first caught on to these ideas in the 1970s, I began tracking my daily activities carefully. It didn't take much tracking to reveal the sad truth: I was spending 90 percent of my time and energy doing things in the three boxes. At best I was spending only 10 percent of my time and energy doing what I really loved to do.

It took me a year or two of dedicated work to get out of my Incompetence Box and Competence Box. For one thing, I had to learn some rudimentary skills of delegating, which definitely didn't come naturally to me. If you're a creative type, which you likely are, you may also have some challenges in learning to delegate. Many creative folks do their work alone and aren't used to telling other people what to do. In my own case, there was no reason I ought to have been any good at it. I'd never had ten seconds of training in any management skills.

The big work, though, was getting out of my Excellence Box. I was a university professor when I first began to focus on the three boxes. The university turned out to be a particularly good laboratory for studying what I call the *Excellence Trap*. No matter how busy you get doing things you're excellent at, you end up feeling unfulfilled, as though you aren't tapping your full creative energy.

I stepped into an Excellence Trap in the very first faculty meeting I attended. Toward the end of the meeting

I got inspired to offer a creative idea about a new course we might offer. The dean beamed at me and said, "Great idea. I'd like you to form a committee to discuss it and report back to us at the next meeting."

Afterward, one of my colleagues, a veteran of many years on the faculty, nudged me and said, "Guess you won't make that mistake again."

I asked him what he meant, and he said, "Whenever anybody comes up with a great idea, the dean appoints a committee to study it. If you're not careful, you'll end up serving on so many committees you won't have time for ideas anymore."

I found his perspective depressing, but he turned out to be absolutely right. Over two decades, I saw many bright professors come into the university and slowly sink into a quagmire of committee meetings and other administrative activities. Inevitably these would turn out to be the same people who groused perpetually about never having time to write or do their pet research.

This problem is not restricted to the academic world; it's a symptom of living in the Excellence Box. If you're excellent at something, people will always be asking you to do more of it. It feels good at first to be wanted and needed by more and more people, but, ultimately, the more things you do in your Excellence Box, the more unfulfilled you end up feeling.

## Out of the Box and onto the Spiral

According to an old joke, the instructions for how to get out of the box are, unfortunately, written on the outside of the box. There's a bit of wisdom in that wit: to get out of a box you're stuck in, you often need to ask someone outside the box for a little help. Even before that, though, you need to decide if you really want to get out of the box.

This brings us again to the subject of commitment. Even if you feel 100 percent committed to your genius and are already living the life of your dreams, take a moment now to bring to life a fresh commitment.

**HANDS-ON ACTIVITY**

The first part of this activity is done in a meditative state, inside your mind. In the second part, you'll need paper and a writing instrument.

To begin, rest for a moment and take your mind off the outside world. Close your eyes or keep them open, as you wish.

Take a few easy, deep breaths and let your body relax.

Try on three different commitments by saying them to yourself in your mind. None of them are right or wrong, good or bad. Your only goal is to discover which one of them feels right to you.

The first commitment is as follows:

*I commit to focusing on my genius one hour a day.*

Repeat the commitment five to ten times in your mind, trying it on as you might try on a new garment to see if it fits.

Here's the second commitment. As before, say this in your mind five to ten times, trying it on to see how it fits:

*I commit to focusing on my genius half my waking hours.*

When you finish, move on to the third commitment, repeating it five to ten times:

*I commit to focusing on my genius all my waking hours.*

When you finish saying the commitments in your mind, pause to reflect on your experience. Which commitment felt most resonant with you?

Pick the most resonant one for the next part of the activity. (In the event that none of the commitments resonate with you right now, come back around to this activity later.)

On your paper, write out in longhand the commitment that feels most resonant to you. Write it out four times, pausing for a couple of easy breaths between repetitions. For example:

*I commit to living in my genius one hour a day.*

*I commit to living in my genius one hour a day.*

*I commit to living in my genius one hour a day.*

*I commit to living in my genius one hour a day.*

Whichever commitment you choose, take note of your body-mind reactions as you write them out.

## Genius Markers

A Genius Marker is a practical, measurable sign that you are living in the Genius Spiral. Here are a few examples:

*I submitted my book to the publisher.*

*I live with a loving partner.*

*I have more in my bank account than I had last year.*

Now that you have expressed your commitment to focusing on your genius for some period of time each day, your next task is to start your journey up the Genius Spiral.

**HANDS-ON ACTIVITY**

**INSTRUCTIONS**

Craft a simple sentence that expresses a marker you could use a year from now to let you know you were living in your genius. Using the graphic on the next page, write a one-year Genius Marker in the first blank space on the spiral.

In the second blank space, write a five-year Genius Marker. For example:

*My coaching hours are fully booked.*

*I teach at least one well-attended seminar a month.*

The third blank space is for what I call a Deathbed Marker. Imagine you are on your deathbed, at the end of a long and successful life. A dear friend drops by and asks you, "Of all the magnificent things you've created in your life, what is the greatest sign that you lived in your genius?"

Craft a sentence that expresses your Deathbed Marker and write it in the third blank space. Put it in the past tense, as if you're looking back over your entire life.

Forty years ago, when I first wondered what my own greatest lifetime sign of genius might be, the answer came to me without hesitation: I created a loving, life-long relationship with a woman who thrilled me every day. At the time, that kind of relationship was just a fantasy to me, but once I got clear on what I really wanted, it wasn't long before I walked into that crowded room in Menlo Park and saw Katie for the first time.

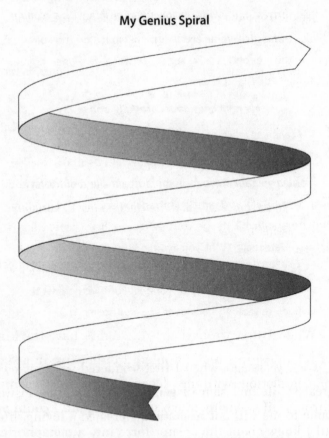

**My Genius Spiral**

I ultimately made a list of five Deathbed Markers for myself. When I imagined looking back over my life from its end point, I chose these as the biggest and best signs I had lived in my genius:

> *I thrived in a loving, lifelong relationship with a woman who thrilled me every day.*

> *I lived in a state of completion with my loved ones, never leaving anything unsaid or overlooked.*

> *I wrote from my heart and created a body of wisdom that could make life easier for others.*

> *I learned as much as I could about the creator force in the universe and did my best to live in harmony with it.*

> *I savored the moments of my life, participating fully in both the painful and the exalted with an open heart.*

When I first wrote that list, I didn't have the kind of relationship I really wanted; I didn't live in a state of completion with my loved ones; I was rushing through life, leaving much unsavored; and I could put all I knew about the creator force into a metaphorical thimble. I was a long way from where I wanted to be. Once I got my Deathbed Markers down in writing, though, my journey afterward became a lifelong ascent up the Genius Spiral until all my dreams eventually came true.

That's what I want for you, too.

# POSTSCRIPT

## *A Farewell Offering*

It has been an honor and a pleasure to carry on this conversation with you. I've endeavored in this book to give you everything I know about how to live a life centered in your genius. If I figure out or come across something else I think would be useful, I'll be sure to let you know.

Writing this book has been an important step for me in fulfilling my life purpose. I first wrote out my chosen purpose for my life in 1977. I've tweaked the wording of it over the years, but it has remained essentially the same as when I first created it:

*I expand in love, abundance, and creativity every day, as I inspire others to do the same through my writing and teaching.*

Up until the moment we choose our own life purpose, we are serving someone else's purpose, sometimes consciously, but more often unconsciously. I've learned through my own journey and from working with people in my office or seminars that there is great joy and satisfaction in fulfilling your own chosen purpose. The reverse is also true: I've experienced the pain of not having my own life purpose, the chaos that comes from bumbling through my days serving someone else's purpose.

## Into Infinity on the Genius Spiral

The Genius Spiral goes up and up and never stops going up. There is no limit to the amount of genius any of us can express. There is also no limit on when we have to stop expressing our genius, either. I want to be expanding in love, abundance, and creativity right up to the moment I exit this magical life.

Some people believe in an afterlife beyond the finite end of their particular bodies. For some, the afterlife is a space of eternal happiness, such as the Christian heaven or the Muslim paradise. For others, it's a new incarnation and another ticket to the karma-go-round.

No afterlife, reincarnation, or heavenly reward has ever held much appeal for me, even in my zealous youth. There is plenty of amazement for me in the awesome fact of existence itself, and all the signs of divinity I need are in the depths of my wife's loving gaze.

Before saying goodbye, I'd like to share a prose poem I wrote one day not long ago when I was out in the garden on a sunny day, thinking about the magnificence of life and the coming adventure of death.

## How I Would Like to Die

I am in my garden, in the big, blue chair under the umbrella. A sweet breeze stirs the air, bringing the scent of orange blossoms down the valley.

I'm listening to the laughter of children from the schoolyard in the distance. It must be recess. Their voices have the happy shriek of liberation.

A flicker catches the corner of my eye. It's a young member of the gecko family that shares our backyard. I pause to admire his sleek design, the sure way his tiny feet grip the rock. He regards me with a still gaze.

From out of the house comes my beloved Katie. Her

movement is poetry, as it has been since the first moment she danced into my life. She comes to rest beside me and beholds me in the eternity of her eyes.

"May I sit with you a while?" she asks.

"Yes," I say, "you may sit with me forever."

I savor a deep breath and feel her presence suffusing me with joy.

Taking her hands in mine, I kiss her passionately and say goodbye, slipping out of time with a big smile on my face.

Thank you for your company throughout the journey of this book. My blessings to you for a lifelong expression of your genius and the good times you harvest as a result.

# APPENDIX A

## The Genius Zone Workbook and Study Guide

### USING THIS GUIDE

### CHAPTER 1: The Essential First Step

- Discussion Topics
- Hands-On Activities
- Activity 1: Heartfelt Committing
- Activity 2: Embodying Recommitment
- Bonus Activity: The Yes Breath

### CHAPTER 2: Mastering the Genius Move

- Discussion Topics
- Hands-On Activities

- Activity Part 1: I Have No Control over _____.
- Activity Part 2: Letting Go, Then Giving Attention to What You Can Control

**CHAPTER 3:** Freeing Up Mind-Space for Genius to Emerge: How to End Your Specific Type of Negative Thinking

- Discussion Topics
- Hands-On Activities
- Activity 1: Learning Fear Melters™: Transforming from Being in Fear to Being Here
- Activity 2: Completing Incompletions
- Bonus Activity: Essence Pace

**CHAPTER 4:** How to Woo Your True Creativity

- Discussion Topics
- Hands-On Activities
- Activity 1: Tuning In to Your Creativity
- Activity 2: Taking Responsibility for What's Blocking Creative Flow
- Activity 3: Discovering Actions That Support Your Creative Flow

**CHAPTER 5:** Three Boxes and a Spiral: A New Way to Organize Your Life in the Genius Zone

- Discussion Topics
- Hands-On Activity

- Activity: Identifying and Getting in Touch with Your Genius

## Using This Guide

This guide is organized to align with the chapters in *The Genius Zone*.

The explorations and activities in this guide offer ways of accentuating and deepening your engagement with your genius. They are designed to be done in order, as they build on each other and the activities found within *The Genius Zone*.

While you don't have to complete the entire book prior to engaging with this guide, be sure to have read each chapter and done each of its Hands-On Activities before you begin the corresponding section in this guide.

### DISCUSSION TOPICS

Discussion topics are offered to support you and your group in initiating and creating a conversation around your experiences with *The Genius Zone*. The length of time in which your group holds a discussion is up to you and your group members, but expected times are listed within this guide.

## HANDS-ON ACTIVITIES

The Hands-On Activities included in this guide complement the book's Hands-On Activities. Have your group bring with them their folders, papers, and writing utensils they used while going through the book, as they will be using some of those items in this guide. Your group members may also have insights or aha moments they will want to write down as they go through the activities.

## Chapter 1: The Essential First Step

### DISCUSSION TOPICS
- What did you notice in your body as you wrote out your commitment statement for ending your negative thinking and liberating your true creativity?

- What do you want to create?

### HANDS-ON ACTIVITIES
Expected time required:
- Activity 1: twenty-five to thirty minutes (includes five to ten minutes of discussion)

- Activity 2: five to six minutes + discussion time of your choosing
- Bonus Activity: twenty-five minutes

## ACTIVITY 1: HEARTFELT COMMITTING

**SUPPLIES**

Everyone will need something to write on and something to write with.

**INSTRUCTIONS**

1. Tell everyone, "Write out your commitment to ending negative thinking and liberating your true creativity. It goes like this: 'I, _____, commit to ending my negative thinking and liberating my true creativity.'"

2. Have your group members get into pairs and bring their commitment statements with them. Once paired, proceed to step 3.

3. Ask the pairings to decide who is Person A and who is Person B.

4. Set a timer for two minutes.

5. Give instructions for the activity:

   a. Person A: Once I say, "Start," you will begin saying your commitment statement out loud, noticing what happens with your breath.

   b. Person A: You will repeat your statement, emphasizing different words and using a variety of inflections and tones.

   c. Person B: you will observe Person A and, when you a notice change in Person A's breathing, invite them to return to easy breathing as they continue to say their commitment statement.

d. After two minutes, you'll hear [a bell] and we'll switch. Please hold your discussion about the exercise until we return to the group.

6. Tell the group to begin. Start your timer.

7. After two minutes [ring a bell] and have them switch. Say something like, "Now Person B will be saying their statement in various ways, while Person A observes Person B's breathing and invites them to return to easy breathing when they notice Person B's breathing isn't easy and flowing."

8. Start your timer again.

**GROUP DISCUSSION**

After both partners have explored, invite the group to reassemble for a five-to-ten-minute discussion about what they noticed. Here are some questions you can try out if the discussion doesn't start on its own:

Did anyone notice their breath dropping out or that they were holding their breath?

When did that happen? Was it during the in breath or out breath?

What sensations were you feeling? Describe those.

What emotions were arising within you?

Did you feel more aliveness the more you said your statement?

## ACTIVITY 2: EMBODYING RECOMMITMENT

### SUPPLIES

Everyone will need something to write on and something to write with.

### INSTRUCTIONS

Nothing negative has to happen for us to recommit to a commitment or goal. Taking action toward a goal is a form of embodying our commitment. In essence, we become a living recommitment.

1. Set a timer for three minutes.

2. Tell the group the following:

   a. In this activity, you'll be writing out your commitment to ending negative thinking and liberating your true creativity as a recommitment. Write it out a number of times.

   b. Each time, as you write your recommitment, notice what arises in your body. Notice what happens with your breathing. What emotions do you feel? Where does this live in your body?

   c. As a reminder, here's what you'll be writing: "I, _____, recommit to ending my negative thinking and liberating my true creativity."

3. Tell the group to begin. Start your timer.

**GROUP DISCUSSION**

Once the timer is done, invite the group to discuss what they noticed.

**BONUS ACTIVITY: THE YES BREATH**

**SUPPLIES**

You will need a computer with audio and speakers and an internet connection.

**INSTRUCTIONS**

This breathing technique supports you being fully present and feeling in flow.

1. Have the group watch Gay's breathing video (ten minutes): https://www.youtube.com/watch?v=Tf9fCWYbOU0

2. Then spend five minutes practicing the techniques in the video.

3. Take a short break.

4. Practice for another five minutes.

**GROUP DISCUSSION**

Invite the group to discuss what they noticed while practicing the Yes Breath.

## Chapter 2: Mastering the Genius Move

DISCUSSION TOPICS

- Describe your experience of playing with the Genius Move. What did you learn?

- Describe your experiences of letting go.

## HANDS-ON ACTIVITIES

Expected time required:

- Activity Part 1: fifteen to twenty minutes

- Activity Part 2: fifteen to eighteen minutes + discussion time of your choosing

### ACTIVITY PART 1: I HAVE NO CONTROL OVER _____.

**SUPPLIES**

Everyone will need their "PERFORM THE GENIUS MOVE WHEN I THINK ABOUT THESE THINGS" sheet of paper and a red writing utensil (pencil, pen, marker, etc.).

**INSTRUCTIONS**

1  Set a timer for five minutes.

2. Tell the group to get out their papers and red writing utensils.

3. Tell the group, "Over the next few minutes, write as many things as you can think of that you have no control over yet try to control."

4. Tell the group to begin. Start your timer.

5. After time is up, have the group bring their supplies with them and get into pairs.

6. Set a timer for five minutes.

7. Once they are in pairs, tell the group the following:

a. Now you are going to alternate between the

two of you, each saying out loud items you have no control over yet try to control. You can choose to say the same item over and over, or you can go through your list.

b. Use this sentence construct for your items: "I have no control over _____." Here's an example: if one of my items is, "If it's a sunny out," I'd say, "I have no control over whether it's sunny out."

c. While your partner is the one speaking, notice if their breathing drops out, and invite easy breathing for them with a statement like, "Let's breathe easy and say that one again."

d. Remember to take turns so each of you has a chance to share. (You can also give them notice at the halfway point to switch if they haven't.)

8. Tell the group to begin. Start your timer.

9. After time is up, have everyone take a short break (one to two minutes) to move their bodies (walk around the room at a comfortable pace, shake, wiggle, etc.) before starting part 2 of this activity.

## ACTIVITY PART 2: LETTING GO, THEN GIVING ATTENTION TO WHAT YOU CAN CONTROL

### SUPPLIES

Everyone needs their list of things they cannot control.

**INSTRUCTIONS**

1. Now have the same pairs get together again and bring their supplies with them.

2. Tell everyone to look over their "THINGS I ABSOLUTELY CANNOT CONTROL" list and to choose the top two or three items that have the most charge for them.

3. Set a timer for five minutes.

4. Ask the pairs to select a Person A and a Person B.

5. Give instructions for Person A (consider giving a demonstration):

   a. Person A, you will be exploring.

   b. Choose one of your top items from your list of things you cannot control.

   c. First you will imagine the item in your hand and grasp it firmly.

   d. Then as you say, "I consciously let go of trying to control [your item]," open your hand and let the item go.

   e. You might try this with each hand.

   f. Keep repeating the process with one item until you feel space in your body, a rush of aliveness and flow.

   g. When you do feel a shift in your body, begin to wonder out loud, "Hmmm . . . I wonder what positive action I can do right away?"

   h. Once you have an action item, make a note of the item and write down your action step.

    i. If you have more time, start this process over with another item you cannot control. And if a new item comes to mind while doing this exercise, go ahead and use that or write it down for later exploration!

    j. And remember, if at any time your breathing stops, just take note and return to easy, full breathing.

6. Give instructions for Person B:

    a. Person B, you will be supporting, noticing, and inviting breath.

    b. First, create a supportive space by getting into the present yourself and finding your own easy breathing. During your partner's entire exploration, do your best to demonstrate easy breathing.

    c. Your job here is to be an active listener, fully available to your partner, paying attention to your partner's breathing and body and generating curiosity in yourself about what's going on for your partner.

    d. When you notice their breath drop out or pause, gently invite them to breathe with something like, "Remember to breathe," or, "I noticed your breath dropped out. Can you bring that back in?"

7. Tell the group to begin. Start your timer.

8. When the timer ends, invite the group to switch roles. Start your timer for five minutes again.

9. After both Partners A and B have had a chance to go, invite the group to take a minute or two to fully enjoy their experience.

> **GROUP DISCUSSION**
>
> Have the group reassemble and ask them what they noticed and what worked best for them for letting go.

## Chapter 3: Freeing Up Mind-Space for Genius to Emerge: How to End Your Specific Type of Negative Thinking

**DISCUSSION TOPICS**

- What was your experience like as you were writing, "I commit to speaking honestly and listening mindfully"?

- What is your experience of loving your negative thoughts, just as they are, like? How does that feel in your body?

**HANDS-ON ACTIVITIES**

Expected time required:

- Activity 1: eighteen to twenty-two minutes + discussion time of your choosing

- Activity 2: twenty to twenty-two minutes + discussion time of your choosing

- Bonus Activity: five to ten minutes + discussion time of your choosing

## ACTIVITY 1: LEARNING FEAR MELTERS™: TRANSFORMING FROM BEING IN FEAR TO BEING HERE

### SUPPLIES

You will need a computer with audio and speakers and an internet connection as well as copies of the enclosed Fear Melters™ handout for your group.

### INSTRUCTIONS

This activity is about supporting you being fully present with your emotions.

1. Watch Katie's Fear Melters™ video (six minutes): https://www.youtube.com/watch?v=pGS2byt4kZ8

2. Then watch Rebecca Folsom's Fear Melters™ Demonstrations (five minutes): https://www .youtube.com/watch?v=vZUnfPLHpg0

3. For one minute have the group practice going from freeze to wiggling or shaking.

4. For one minute have the group practice going from flee stance to sumo stance.

5. For one minute have the group practice going from fight movements to oozing movements.

6. For one minute have the group practice going from faint scoops to love scoops.

7. Now have the group play with combining the Fear Melters™ for one to two minutes. Invite folks from the group who want to create a combo and demonstrate it to the group to do so while the rest of the group tries it on for themselves.

## ACTIVITY 2: COMPLETING INCOMPLETIONS

**SUPPLIES**

Everyone will need a piece of paper and something to write with.

**INSTRUCTIONS**

1. Set a timer for five minutes.

2. First tell the group, "While doing this next activity, anytime you feel scared, do some Fear Melters™."

3. Next, tell everyone, "Make a list of all the things you can think of that are incomplete in your life. It doesn't matter how big or how small the item is, just write it down. Here are some examples:

   a. Conversations with people you've been putting off

   b. Mail you haven't gone through

   c. Paying a bill

   d. Calling that friend you love and letting them know you love them"

4. Tell the group to begin. Start the timer.

5. When the timer ends tell everyone, "Now you'll be going through your list and writing next to each incompletion what action step you are going to take to either gain completion or begin completing that item."

6. Tell the group to begin. Start the timer for another five minutes.

7. When the timer ends, set another timer for five

minutes and tell everyone to write a "by when" for each action step. This is "by when" they will do that action. Set the timer for another five minutes.

## GROUP DISCUSSION

After time's up, have the group reassemble and discuss what they noticed.

## BONUS ACTIVITY: ESSENCE PACE

### SUPPLIES

Everyone will need their body and space to walk around.

### INSTRUCTIONS

This activity is about finding your natural pace, in which you feel in flow, easy, and abundant.

1. Have the group tune in to their breathing and do a minute or so of easy breathing.
2. Then, for about one to two minutes, invite them to walk around at a pace in which they are still breathing easy.
3. Then, for one to two minutes, invite them to—in a friendly way—start speeding up and slowing down, noticing when their breathing changes (speeds up, stops) and when space appears to be opening and closing.
4. Next, for about two minutes, invite them to continue changing their speed until they find a walking speed or speeds at which they are moving about the room with ease, breathing easily, feeling fully present, and

noticing that the room feels more spacious to them. That's their essence pace.

5. Have the group come to a rest and discuss what they noticed.

## Chapter 4: How to Woo Your True Creativity

### DISCUSSION TOPICS

- What did you discover as you explored wondering?

- What were your top-three wonder-questions?

- What did you discover as you explored cultivating relationships that support your creativity?

### HANDS-ON ACTIVITIES

Expected time required:

- Activity 1: twelve to fifteen minutes + discussion time of your choosing

- Activity 2: twelve to fifteen minutes + discussion time of your choosing

- Activity 3: eight to ten minutes + discussion time of your choosing

### ACTIVITY 1: TUNING IN TO YOUR CREATIVITY

#### SUPPLIES

Everyone will need a piece of paper and something to write with.

# APPENDIX A

**INSTRUCTIONS**

1. Tell the group, "In this activity you'll be exploring what it's like to be in your creative flow. Write down your answers to the following questions."

2. Now read these questions to the group, allowing about a minute for them to answer each.

   a. What does it feel like to be in your creative flow? For some people, they lose track of time or time seems to expand. Others feel spaciousness in their bodies and a sense of joy and ease.

   b. How does it feel in your body to be in your creative flow?

   c. While you're in your creative flow, how do you experience your energy and aliveness? What is your mental state like?

   d. How do others experience you while you're in your creative flow? What kind of feedback do you receive from being in your creative flow?

3. Next, invite the group to share and talk about what they discovered. Also invite the group to write down any insights or ideas that arise for them during the discussion.

4. Next, set a timer for five minutes.

5. Tell the group, "Now you'll be exploring and writing down ways that you get into your creative flow or ways that support you being in your creative flow. For some people, meditation sets the stage for creativity to flow, for others it's moving, and for others it's something else. What

are the ways you reliably invite your own flow of creativity?"

6. Tell the group to begin. Start the timer.

**GROUP DISCUSSION**

Once the timer is done, invite the group to share their discoveries. Invite the group to write down for themselves any insights or ideas that arise for them during the discussion.

## ACTIVITY 2: TAKING RESPONSIBILITY FOR WHAT'S BLOCKING CREATIVE FLOW

**SUPPLIES**

Everyone will need a piece of paper and something to write with.

**INSTRUCTIONS**

1. Tell the group, "In this activity you'll be exploring what's blocking your creative flow."

2. Tell the group to get into pairs.

3. Then tell them to choose who will be Person A and Person B.

4. Set a timer for five minutes.

5. Tell them the following:

   a. Person B, you will be interviewing Person A and supporting their exploration. If at any time you notice either of you not breathing, invite easy breathing and Fear Melters™.

165

b. First you are going to ask Person A to complete this sentence: "I would express my creativity fully if _____."

c. After they complete it, say something like, "I hear that you don't have time to spend creating. What's underneath that?"

d. Keep asking, ". . . and under that?" until your partner lands firmly on what's underneath their stories. When they do, invite them to feel all their feelings, breathing, moving, and loving their full experience, including any judgments or stories they might have about what they are experiencing.

e. If your partner is getting stuck, try one of these invitations:

*Tell me more.*

*What interests you most about that?*

*Then what happened?*

6. Next tell Person A the following:

a. Person A, your job is to breathe, answer the questions, and, when you notice yourself feeling scared or stuck, do Fear Melters™ and generate a whole-body "hmmm."

7. Tell the group to begin. Start the timer.

8. After the timer is done, set another timer and have the partners switch roles. Read the instructions again if needed.

9. Tell the group to begin. Start the timer.

**GROUP DISCUSSION**

When the timer is done, invite the group to write down any aha moments or insights and to share their discoveries.

## ACTIVITY 3: DISCOVERING ACTIONS THAT SUPPORT YOUR CREATIVE FLOW

**SUPPLIES**

Everyone will need a piece of paper and something to write with.

**INSTRUCTIONS**

1. Set a timer for five minutes.
2. Tell the group, "In this activity you will be exploring physical, tangible actions you can take that embody you wooing and expressing your true creativity. Like Gay and Katie going to the Met in New York and appreciating art, how and when do you or could you woo your creativity by appreciating and visiting it every chance you get?"
3. Here are some more questions to get you started:
   a. For making time for expressing your true creativity: Can you make a date to show up with your creativity each day, even for just fifteen minutes? If you're already doing fifteen minutes, what amount of time could you increase that to? When we cherish a relationship, we make time each day to

connect with the person. What can you do on a daily basis to connect with your creativity?

b. What are some ways you can appreciate your creativity?

c. What can you do that supports your creative flow? This could be to dance, move, meditate, brainstorm ideas with a friend, play with a pet, or something else.

4. Tell the group to write down whatever comes to mind for them.

5. Tell the group to begin. Then start the timer.

6. Tell the group, "Now take a moment to choose one action you can take and commit to doing it every day for the next week. Once that week is up, see if you can do them for even longer. Once you've integrated that action, add more, but just start with one and see what happens."

**GROUP DISCUSSION**

Invite the group to share about their experiences doing this activity and what they plan to do. Invite anyone who wants to stand up to do so and to say their action step out loud for the group to witness.

## Chapter 5: Three Boxes and a Spiral: A New Way to Organize Your Life in the Genius Zone

### DISCUSSION TOPICS

- What did you choose for your commitment to spending time in your zone of genius?

- What Genius Markers did you choose to serve as measurables for spending time in your zone of genius?
- What did you choose for your five Deathbed Markers?

**HANDS-ON ACTIVITY**

Expected time required:

- Twenty-four to twenty-six minutes + discussion time of your choosing

---

### ACTIVITY: IDENTIFYING AND GETTING IN TOUCH WITH YOUR GENIUS

**SUPPLIES**

Everyone will need a piece of paper and something to write with.

**INSTRUCTIONS**

1. Set a timer for ten minutes.

2. Tell the group, "In this activity you'll be exploring your genius. You'll be answering the following questions, writing down your answers (you'll need them in the next part of the activity):

   a. What is my unique ability?

   b. What do I most love to do?

   c. What produces the highest ratio of abundance per time spent?

   d. What work do I do that doesn't seem like work?"

3. Tell the group to begin. Then start the timer.

4. When the timer ends have the group pair up, bringing their answers with them as well as something to write with so they can take notes.

5. Have each pair decide who will be Person A and who will be Person B.

6. Set a timer for five minutes.

7. Tell the group, "Person A will be the first explorer, and Person B will be the first co-explorer. Person A will read their answers to the questions we just answered, and Person B will support their further exploration by asking these questions:

   a. Do any of these actually belong in the Excellence or Competence box?

   b. What's the common theme weaving through your answers?

   c. Which of these are your actual genius, and which of them are ways you express your genius?"

8. Tell the group to begin. Then start the timer.

9. After the timer is done, set another five-minute timer and invite the group to switch roles.

10. Tell the group to begin. Then start the timer.

**GROUP DISCUSSION**

After the timer is done have the group write down any aha moments and discuss what they discovered.

# APPENDIX B

## Your Completions Checklist

To be incomplete about a person or experience means that you still think about the experience and have recurring body sensations related to the experience. There is awesome power in completing the loose ends in our lives.

Examples:

**A BROKEN** shed door you noticed six months ago but haven't gotten around to fixing

**A PROJECT** you stopped short of finishing

**A LOVED** one you haven't connected with in a while

When you're incomplete about something, it causes specific things to happen in your body and mind:

**GUILT**

**SHAME**

**DENIAL**

**SADNESS**

**ANGER**

**FEAR**

As you go through the following checklist, notice any of the above or other reactions in your body and mind.

❏ Do you experience trespasses—instances when you let people intrude upon your boundaries to the point of causing you pain or distress?

❏ Do you experience withholds—instances when you choose to hide from others what you said, felt, did, or thought?

❏ Do you experience moments of inaction—instances when you choose not to follow your intuition to take an action, missing out on an opportunity to be authentic and complete?

❏ Do you persist in behavior you find to be unacceptable, such as consuming problematic amounts of caffeine, sugar, television, drugs, or alcohol?

❏ Have you told the people closest to you that you love them within the past week?

❏ Have you communicated and made amends with everyone you have hurt or seriously upset in your life?

❏ Do you always tell the truth, no matter what?

❏ Do you let go of relationships that drag you down?

❏ Are you fully caught up with email, paperwork, and phone calls?

❏ Do you quickly correct miscommunications and misunderstandings when they occur?

❏ Do you have significant uncommunicated feelings or issues with people from your past?

❏ Do you have a best friend or a soul mate?

❏ Are your personal and business files, papers, and receipts organized so they can be easily located?

❏ Are you consistently on time?

❏ Is your car in good condition?

❏ Is your house neat and clean?

❏ Do you have adequate time, space, and freedom in your life to pursue creative passions?

❏ Do you have any articles or things, such as clothing, in your house or in storage that you would like to be rid of?

❏ Are you putting up with anything about your home or work environment that you wish you could change?

❏ Do you pay your bills on time?

❏ Do you know how much you need to be financially independent and have a plan to get there?

❏ Have your tax returns been filed and all taxes been paid?

❏ Do you currently live within your means?

❏ Do you have any unpaid parking tickets, taxes, alimony, or child support?

❏ Do you have good health insurance?

❏ Is your will up to date?

## COMPLETIONS: AN ONGOING PROCESS

No checklist could ever be complete, because completions are an ongoing process in daily life. On a moment-by-moment basis as we move through life, it's essential that we stay vigilant for incompletions. Use the checklist as a starting point; it will give you several key areas to focus on. As I mentioned earlier, my own list of incompletions ran to twelve pages. At first my list seemed daunting, but my mood lifted as I took care of my incompletions one day at a time. The good news, though, is that almost everything you are incomplete about is completable. Many, in fact, can be completed in ten seconds with a communication such as, "I just want to let you know how much I appreciate you."

# Acknowledgments

First a deep bow of gratitude to Epictetus, whose wisdom has illuminated so many millions of lives over the past two thousand years. It was in his *Enchiridion* (*Handbook*) that I first encountered the central idea of this book.

Three generations of participants in our seminars for professionals, now several thousand in number, have contributed immeasurably to my understanding of personal change and relationship transformation. I'm grateful to our professional community and the larger community of those who use our tools to enjoy more love, creativity, and abundance in their lives.

Thanks to my friends who serve as first readers, giving me feedback on my writings in their early, unpolished form. Special thanks to Geneen Roth, Kenny Loggins, Neale Donald Walsch, Carol Kline, Stephen Simon, Jim Selman, and Zhena Muzyka for their contributions over many years. I'm grateful also for the contributions of Melanie Bates, who assisted with the launch and creation of the Genius Zone Workbook and Study Guide.

I've been richly blessed to be supported by my amazing team of agents: Sandy Dijkstra, Bonnie Solow, and Bill Gladstone representing both fiction and nonfiction, along with Andrea Cavallaro and Rachel Miller on the television and film side.

Finally, to Katie, my mate and best friend for four decades, my gratitude is absolute. One of the great pleasures of my life is reading aloud to you what I've written during the day. Even though I've read thousands of pages to you over the years, I still get just as excited to hear your feedback as the first time I read a fresh page to you in 1980. Thank you for a lifetime of generous listening.

# About the Author

Mariana Schulze

GAY HENDRICKS, Ph.D., has served for more than forty years as one of the major contributors to the fields of relationship transformation and body-mind therapies. He is a *New York Times* bestselling author and his books include *Conscious Loving* and *The Big Leap*.